FOUNDATIONS CURRICULUM

VENTURE UP

SPIRITUAL PRACTICES

Volume 1, Book 2

Travelogue

Ronald K. Brown and Amy Tucker Summers

EquippedChurch.es, a publishing ministry extension of Brentwood Baptist Church

VENTURE UP: Spiritual Practices, Volume 1, Book 2

This travelogue is designed for use by adults to record and assess their individual spiritual journey to Christlikeness

PROJECT LEADERSHIP TEAM
J. Steven Layton, Concept & Strategy
Roger Severino, Content Design, Scope & Sequence
Norma J. Goldman, Project Manager

EDITORIAL STAFF
Ronald K. Brown, Content Writer
Amy T. Summers, Content Writer
David T. Seay, General Editor
Linda L. Still, Teaching Plan Writer

Printed in the United States of America
ISBN 978-1-941231-01-2

To view or purchase Foundation Curriculum Resources visit us at www.equippedchurch.es

To learn more about the JourneyOn Network of Churches and/or JourneyOn Resources email us at info@journeyondiscipleship.com or visit us on the web at www.journeyondiscipleship.com.

NOTHING GETS BETTER BY ITSELF

Nothing gets better by itself. Without some kind of intention, some kind of focused energy, nothing will change. We won't improve our health without being intentional about exercise and nutrition. We won't get better at playing a musical instrument or any sports without practice. You have to decide you want something to change, decide what action is required for that change to happen and then, you have to act. There are no exceptions.

And this includes our spiritual lives. Too many of us have become victims of shallow theology when it comes to growing as a disciple of Christ. For one thing, many of us don't know we're supposed to grow. Yet, the Scriptures are clear on this point, especially the apostle Paul. Once we're born again, Christ calls us to grow again. Another misconception many of us have is that growing in Christ is something that happens to us without us having to do anything. A lot of us think that sitting in church is like being put in a microwave oven. Ding! Now, we're a mature Christian.

There are many more misconceptions and false teachings about this, but you get my point. Like everything else in our lives, nothing happens to us spiritually without intentional and thoughtful action. For thousands of years, Christians have been trying to find the best ways to grow closer to Christ. The results of these efforts are a handful of disciplines we call the Spiritual Practices. Prayer, Bible study, and fasting are just a few of the intentional actions Christians have found, that when done, bring us closer to Christ. The purpose of this study is to introduce these time tested practices to you and help you bring their intentionality into your own life.

When Jesus called His disciples, He called them to come and follow. That same call has come to us. Jesus will lead the way, but we'll have to walk fast to keep up with Him.

Michael Glenn, D. Min.
Senior Pastor, Brentwood Baptist Church
Brentwood, Tennessee

INTRODUCTION TO THE TRAVELOGUE

The travelogue for Spiritual Practices is designed to be a companion to an individual's Bible study experience. It will help learners delve more deeply into certain spiritual habits like Bible study, prayer, worship, stewardship, sharing our faith, silence and solitude, and sacrifice.

The travelogue is designed to accompany learners on their spiritual journey toward becoming more like Jesus, which is God's great intent for His children (see Romans 8:29; 2 Cor. 3:18; 1 John 3:1-3). These spiritual habits are not legalistic duties, or a means to score spiritual "brownie points." We are saved by grace alone and can add nothing to Christ's finished work on the cross. But this doesn't mean the Christian life is passive. God has provided certain "means of grace" that allow us to participate with His work in our lives. Spiritual practices put us in a position to allow God to work in us and transform us more into the image of His Son.

There are different types of journeys. Some are ones that we take with friends or family, while others are adventures we pursue on our own. The travelogue is designed to be used either way. Learners may dive into these spiritual practices by themselves, so the journal is designed to stand on its own. Others may gather a group of friends, going through the travelogue together, sharing insights each has gained during private times of engaging the material. Finally, we have developed teaching plans that allow these lessons to be taught in a more traditional format, such as a LIFE Group or Sunday School class.

The travelogue is designed to encourage practicing at least four different spiritual disciplines in each lesson. First, learners engage a text of Scripture, thus practicing Bible study. Secondly, we have included a memory verse for each lesson to encourage the habit of Bible memorization. Third, journaling will be part of the experience as learners write out their thoughts in engaging the material. Finally, prayer is an essential part of this experience as we prayerfully reflect on how God is speaking to us.

Each travelogue (Book 1: *Venture In* and Book 2: *Venture Up*) introduces 12 spiritual practices. By going through both books, learners will study 24 different habits. It would be easy to walk away burdened with trying to maintain all of these, rather than finding them a source of spiritual growth and freedom. *Remember, the goal is not to practice all the disciplines but to become more like Jesus.*

We hope you will find these practices to be a true source of joy and encouragement as you take your next steps on the journey.

Happy travels!

TABLE OF CONTENTS

VENTURE UP: *Spiritual Practices* — *Volume 1, Book 2*

THE PURPOSE OF SPIRITUAL PRACTICES CURRICULUM

Norma J. Goldman

Perhaps you, like I, have been studying curriculum for decades. You may have hoped and dreamed that your studies would bring you closer to God, to be more like Him. You likely have developed a deep appreciation for the things of God, the stories of His interaction with mankind in the grand metanarrative of Scripture, and a hope for what is yet to come.

But isn't what you yearn for most is a richer spiritual life, a deeper understanding of God and a relationship with Him? These yearnings can be satisfied in *practicing* the spiritual disciplines because they are essential to experiencing God. This sounds like a radical statement—and it is because in a real sense, to live out the disciplines is to move toward Christlikeness, breaking free of slavery to "religious duties."

The goal of this curriculum is not simply to educate, to learn the facts so to speak, but to bring about life-change, transformation. And we believe that not just studying, but *practicing* the spiritual disciplines will do just that!

We cannot change ourselves through willpower; trying to do so is fruitless—impossible really. But in practicing the disciplines, we *put ourselves in a place* where God can transform us. This does not happen by accident; it is a conscious personal choice. It is only His power that brings about the change, the transformation we long for.

Practicing the disciplines is not reserved for super saints; it is designed for people like you and me who are doing life—raising families, building businesses, working through relationships and the problems of everyday life. Spiritual disciplines, like prayer, meditation, solitude and celebration bring balance to our lives even as we live in an unbalanced world!

Some of the disciplines focus inwardly, such as meditation and prayer so that we can intentionally search out those habits, thoughts and practices that need to be changed. Others, like simplicity and service, move us to make our world a better place. It is the corporate disciplines of confession, worship, and celebration that move us closer to each other and to God. This curriculum was designed with you in mind, to bless you and to prosper your journey toward becoming more like Him!

HOW ARE THESE LESSONS ARRANGED?

Roger Severino

In case you did not buy both books in this series, you should know that this spiritual practices curriculum is divided into two books: *Venture In* and *Venture Up*. Each book contains 13 lessons and addresses 12 different spiritual disciplines.

Venture In serves as an invitation to begin the journey, perhaps at the trailhead. These lessons are for both the novice and the experienced, but it begins with foundational teachings on the spiritual practices. *Venture Up*, the second book, targets either those who have completed the first book, or those who feel they have covered sufficient ground and are ready to venture up further.

Since each book covers 12 different spiritual practices, the math adds up to 24 lessons on these habits. Why did we pick these particular ones? How are they arranged? How did we decide on a scope and sequence for this material?

First, we began by listing all the different spiritual practices we could imagine. We looked at various resources available, and attempted to see how different books addressed various disciplines. Next, we realized that many of these practices could be collected into different categories. In the end, we arrived at six: Bible, Communion with God, Character, Stewardship (holistic, not simply money), Corporate disciplines, and Outward disciplines.

Next, we were able to identify four different practices that fell into these six categories. So, for example, in the "Bible" category we have Reading, Study, Memorization, and Meditation. As a general rule, we attempted to move from the basic to the more challenging. Of course, we made a judgment call on these, and you may or may not agree with our decisions on laying out the spectrum.

Finally, we decided it may be more helpful and balanced to study one from each category at a time, rather than simply focusing in on one category. You will notice from the Table of Contents, then, that you have one lesson from each of the six areas, and then you repeat the six areas again at the next level. *Venture In* (Book 1) covers two topics within each broader category, and *Venture Up* (Book 2) does the same. So, under "Bible," you will have Reading and Studying in Book 1, and Memorization and Meditation in Book 2.

Our hope and prayer is that we have provided a resource that will help you engage the Scriptures and these spiritual practices in a way that will enrich your walk with Christ, and move you along your journey in becoming more like Him!

CHAPTER 1

BIBLE MEMORIZATION

HOW CAN IT HELP?

WHY STUDY THIS LESSON? Memorizing Scripture allows us to carry God's Word in our hearts and minds so that we can fight against sin and reflect on God's truths.

BACKGROUND PASSAGE	FOCAL PASSAGE	MEMORY VERSE
PSALM 119	PSALM 119:9-16	PSALM 119:11

FURTHER UP, FURTHER IN

As *The Chronicles of Narnia* come to an end, C.S. Lewis' characters find themselves traveling in "a deeper country" where everything looks a little different and means vastly more. Though all are delighted to be in that place, they are not content to stay where they are, and urge one another to, "Come further up, come further in!"[1] Perhaps you have already discovered through foundational spiritual practices in *Venture In* the absolute delight of journeying toward a Christ-centered life. Now you have the opportunity to progress "further up and further in" and experience an increasingly deeper reality of life in Jesus. These studies will guide you to *Venture Up* by exploring and applying 12 additional spiritual practices that will put you in a position to hear from God and allow Him to progressively form, conform, and transform you into the image of His Son.

FURTHER INTO THE WORD

In your journey toward becoming more like Christ you have discovered the importance of God's Word and perhaps are settling into the regular practice of reading the Bible and participating in small-group Bible study.

Based on Psalm 119:9-16 below, how can I venture up in my understanding and application of God's Word?

> *9 How can a young man keep his way pure? By keeping Your word. 10 I have sought You with all my heart; don't let me wander from Your commands. 11 I have treasured Your word in my heart so that I may not sin against You. 12 LORD, may You be praised; teach me Your statutes. 13 With my lips I proclaim all the judgments from Your mouth. 14 I rejoice in the way revealed by Your decrees as much as in all riches. 15 I will meditate on Your precepts and think about Your ways. 16 I will delight in Your statutes; I will not forget Your word* (Ps. 119:9-16).

I still have a simple wooden plaque that I made in Vacation Bible School decades ago. Pasted on the lightly varnished piece of wood is a picture of a small boy looking out a window with the caption, "For He careth for you. 1 Peter 5:7." This Bible verse, the first I remember memorizing, is etched in my mind. It has surfaced many times over the years to remind me of God's love and to encourage me in times of difficulty or challenge. When I have failed the Lord, I am reminded, "He careth for you." When others have been angry with and hurt me, I recall, "He careth for you." I decided to follow Christ because I was convinced that Jesus died on the cross because, "He careth for you."

What is the first Bible verse you recall memorizing?

Write down some benefits you have gained by having that word from God in your memory.

Psalm 119:9-16 identifies three benefits you can derive from memorizing Scripture. By treasuring God's Word in your heart and mind you can resist sin, repeat God's truths, and rejoice in God and His ways.

I CAN RESIST SIN (Ps. 119:9-11)

Psalm 119, the longest chapter in the Bible, celebrates the beauty and authority of God's Word that provides practical instructions for living. The issue of how to live a life that honors the Lord is not just for **a young man** (v. 9), for we all live in a culture that tempts us to **wander** (v.10) off God's path. The Hebrew word translated "wander" comes from a word that means to sin inadvertently, unknowingly, or unconsciously. It's like getting lost while driving in an unfamiliar city. You did not set out to get lost; it happened through one inadvertent turn after another until you were unaware of your location. The psalmist didn't want such a thing to happen in his life; so, he asked for the Lord's intervention and made some very intentional decisions.

What is tempting you at this point in your life to wander from God's good paths?

How are you dealing with those temptations?

A dictionary defines **pure** (v. 9) as being free from pollutants, moral fault, or guilt. But the word translated "pure" in the Bible is used in the moral sense of being and staying clean, translucent, or innocent. That sounds so much like perfection that we may conclude the only answer to the psalmist's question in verse 9 is, "A young man can't and neither can I." But the psalmist did not think it an impractical question or impossible achievement.

What are some intentional decisions you can make to live in ever-increasing purity?

Believers can intentionally continue walking in God's pure ways **by keeping** His Word. The word "keeping" means guarding, observing, or heeding, all of which imply obedience. Because He is the supreme sovereign God worthy of all praise, submission, and obedience, His Word is to be obeyed. Because He is trustworthy, all-knowing, all-powerful, filled with loving-kindness and compassion, His Word can be obeyed.

We can obey God's Word when we seek the Lord by concentrating, investigating, and inquiring of Him. This is an intensely personal and fully involved search, investing all feelings, emotions, intellect, and will into knowing and obeying God so that we do not wander from His commands. If we had the chance to read Scripture every time we needed encouragement or guidance we might do a fairly decent job of not wandering from God's path. But we don't usually have the immediate opportunity to pull out a Bible when another driver cuts us off or a child sasses us. That's why it is so beneficially valuable to intentionally treasure God's Word in our hearts. To treasure is to store up or to hide in a secret place. When we hide away in the deepest recesses of our being all the Lord says to us *for teaching, for rebuking, for correction, for training in righteousness* (2 Tim. 3:16), His truths and promises become assimilated into who we are. Memorizing God's Word empowers us to recall and repeat it to resist sin's temptation.

What difference might it make in my day if Bible verses were the first thoughts that popped into my mind during tests and temptations?

So, one benefit of memorizing Scripture is always having the Lord's Word available to guard and protect us from sin. Memorizing Scripture fills our minds with pure thoughts which lead to pure actions. None of us is going to behave perfectly every day; we all stumble on life's journey. But when our minds and hearts are increasingly filled with God's Word, we are guided around sin's potholes and prevented from wandering off the road that leads to Christlikeness.

I CAN REPEAT GOD'S TRUTHS (Ps. 119:12-13)

The psalmist asked the LORD to **teach me Your statutes** (v. 12), a synonym for the Word or revelation from God. Learning from the Lord is far more than an academic exercise, review of interesting case studies, or analysis of hypothetical situations in light of a few Bible verses. It is a spiritual practice; engaging the Lord through the dynamic of the Holy Spirit who opens up the meaning of His Word so it enlightens our minds and warm our hearts (Luke 24:27-32).

God does not funnel information or understanding into our minds in some supernatural way devoid of individual engagement. Teaching and learning always stand in tandem. Learning calls for someone to teach; teaching assumes someone will learn. The psalmist was offering himself up as a learner willing to be taught, submitting himself to the authority of the Teacher. When we accept Christ's call to follow Him we are choosing to be disciples who submit to the authority of Jesus as our Master and Teacher so we can be taught by and learn from Him (Matt. 7:28-29).

Read Ephesians 4:20-24 in your Bible. What is the desired result of being taught by and learning from Jesus?

What encourages a person to want to learn? Perhaps you know someone who has lots of knowledge about a topic which has no practical value unless the person appears on a TV quiz show. Most of us don't want to be just trivia experts; we are much more pragmatic than that. We want information, knowledge, and understanding that prepare us for a task, enable us to deal with a particular challenge, and equip us to lead or influence others to accomplish a common objective. As followers of Christ, what we have learned about Him and been taught by Him is for the purpose of moving us toward Christlikeness.

The psalmist affirmed he would **proclaim** (v. 13) all God had declared, meaning he would recount and repeat what he had been taught as a way of reinforcing the message to himself. Have you ever crammed for and aced an exam, but then forgot everything you'd remembered so well for that test? That happens when we do not continue to use and apply that information in our daily lives. It's not going to adversely affect your life if you can no longer remember details and dates of some historic event. However what God has spoken is too important to be neglected or forgotten. That's why we intentionally repeat the Word of the Lord over and over to ourselves for our own hearing and learning. The more we speak God's Word out loud and the more we live God's Word out in the world, the more it will become a treasured part of our very being. The result is divine transformation so that the personality and deeds of Jesus naturally flow out of us where we live, work, and play.

The more we treasure God's Word in our hearts the more His words of truth will flow from our lips. We can share what we have been taught with others so they too might experience the powerful, penetrating effects of Scripture. Our witness and ministry are strengthened by being able to accurately repeat what the Bible says. Quoting Scripture from memory indicates how important it is to us. Furthermore, our proclamation is shown to be more than personal opinion or a presentation learned in a witnessing class. Rather it is a message straight from God's heart to our hearts. That's a message others will listen to.

So here is another reason for memorizing Scripture. We always have a Word from the Lord with us—a Word we can repeat to ourselves when we need a reminder of God's faithfulness and a Word we can repeat to others as we witness and minister to them.

Pray, asking God to:

- **Lay on your heart a person to whom He wants you to speak His Word of truth.**
- **Give you a specific verse(s) He wants you to repeat to that person.**
- **Give you the desire and discipline to memorize that verse so you can repeat it when the time is right.**

I CAN REJOICE (Ps. 119:14-16)

Are you looking for a reason to rejoice? The psalmist experienced full joy in keeping, treasuring, learning, and sharing God's Word. **Rejoice** (v. 14) is more than being happy or cheerful. It is to exult or display the greatest joy. In Scripture, the Lord has **revealed** His **way** which means we can know with all assurance the journey, direction, and course of life that is His very best for us. That surely is reason to rejoice. In fact, the psalmist declared he had found reason to rejoice in the Lord's Word **as much as in all riches**. He loved the Word more than the world's affluence.

Identify something that brings you great joy. Complete the statement: I rejoice in the Lord's Word as much as in

________________________________.

Can that statement truthfully be said about you? If so, why? If not, how can it become more of a statement that describes your priorities?

Since having the Bible stored away in our very being results in great joy, it makes perfect sense for us to intentionally and regularly **meditate** on the Lord's **precepts** (v. 15), which comes from a word that refers to orders related to ethical living. To meditate is to ponder, to think about. In some circles meditation is associated with emptying one's mind as an act of internal purification. Not so here. To meditate on the Word from the Lord is to fill our mind with His Word and ponder its implications for our lives.

Why might meditation on God's Word result in memorization of those words?

The Bible, contrary to some false perceptions, is not a burdensome book of rules and legalistic checklists. We can, like the psalmist, know the overflowing joy and **delight** (v. 16) in being liberated and enlightened by God's Word. "Delight" suggests that which is pleasing and amusing, not in the sense of being frivolous but as being so delightfully satisfying that it makes a person feel good all over. When we delight in God's Word we determine to **not forget** it. We daily choose to not ignore the Bible's instructions by failing to remember it or pay attention to it either by intentional rebellion or unintentional default. Why would we even consider doing so, given the potential, power, and promise the Word offers to those who internalize it in their hearts, give expression to it with their lips, and meditate on it in their minds? Here is one last reason the psalmist offered for memorizing Scripture: it brings joy to the heart that exceeds the joy found in any other thing in life.

Recall a time when remembering and reflecting on a memorized Bible passage brought you great joy.

THE PRACTICE IN ACTION

IN JESUS' LIFE

Spiritual practices are an effective means of grace God uses to transform us into the image of Christ because they are practices Jesus engaged in when He walked this earth. After Jesus was baptized the Spirit led Him into the wilderness to be tempted. The Lord's victory over temptation demonstrates His unique sinless character and reinforces the power, strength, and guidance that is available when God's Word is hidden in the heart and mind. Satan used all kinds of tricks to tempt Jesus to take the easy way rather than God's perfect way. Jesus responded to each scheme by quoting Scripture. His obvious memorization and internalization of large portions of the Old Testament empowered Him to resist Satan's temptations and to continue traveling His journey obediently to the cross. His sacrificial death ultimately resulted in full joy not just for the Lord but also for all who trust in Him.

Read Matthew 4:1-11. Which verse that Jesus quoted would best empower me to resist sin, repeat a truth, or rejoice in God and why?

IN MY LIFE

When it comes to memorizing Scripture some people defeat themselves before they ever try, declaring they can't memorize. Nothing is impossible with God. Since He wants you to experience all the benefits of having His Word in your heart and mind, He will give you the power to memorize it. Memorizing Scripture takes work and discipline but it's eternally rewarding. When you intentionally commit to the spiritual practice of Bible memorization you gain countless treasures, including divine power to resist sin, repeat God's truths, and rejoice in and with God.

Try some of these strategies that can help you hide God's Word in your heart:

- Select verses and passages to memorize that speak God's truth to a specific situation in your life. Make that verse a treasure by reflecting on its benefits in helping you resist sin, remember God's promises, or rejoice in His faithfulness. Each session in this spiritual practices study has a designated memory verse that can help you reflect and internalize each practice you will explore. As you progress, consider increasing the length of the passages you set to memory. Consider passages like the Ten Commandments (Ex. 20:2-17), the Beatitudes (Matt. 5:3-12), Psalm 23, Isaiah 40:28-31, Lamentations 3:22-24, John 3:16-18, Romans 3:21-26, and 1 Corinthians 13.

- Write the verse(s) on a 3-by-5-inch card (preferably spiral bound) or on a notes app so you can keep it with you at all times. Pause after writing each phrase and really reflect on its meaning.
- Say the memory verse out loud several times, including its reference. Continue repeating it, phrase by phrase, until you can say it fluidly without mistakes. Repeat the process the next day and the next. Mix it up by repeating it with a different cadence or accent—that might seem silly but it's effective.
- Sing the verse to the tune of a hymn, chorus, or nursery rhyme; that works for adults as well as it does for children.
- Refer to the verse(s) often during the day to reinforce it in your memory. Occasionally go back and review verses you've already memorized so you won't forget them.
- Find a memory partner to encourage and hold you accountable. Meet or call regularly to recite the verse(s) you've been memorizing and review past memory verses.
- Give yourself an occasional test. Select a Bible reference of a verse you've memorized and strive to write out the verse word for word.
- The most effective way to memorize the Word is to live it. Intentionally live the principles in the verses you're working to memorize. When that verse becomes part of you, it will stay with you, and then God's truths and Christ's nature is what will come out of you.

What verse(s) do you want to memorize?

What strategies will you use to hide that portion of God's Word in your heart?

---

[1] C.S. Lewis, *The Chronicles of Narnia: The Last Battle* (New York: HarperCollins Publishers, 1984), 196.

CHAPTER 2

SOLITUDE AND SILENCE

IS IT REALLY POSSIBLE?

WHY STUDY THIS LESSON? Jesus set the example of going to deserted places to escape the demands and distractions of this life in order to hear from the Father and commune with Him.

BACKGROUND PASSAGE	FOCAL PASSAGE	MEMORY VERSE
MARK 1:29-45	MARK 1:35-39	PSALM 46:10

TAKE A DEEP BREATH

Doug is a physician, married father of four, chairman of deacons at his church, and children's Sunday morning worship leader. His days are dominated by hospital calls and office visits and his evenings filled with church obligations or kid's activities. All these worthy responsibilities leave little time for Doug to nurture his relationship with the Lord. What could have been a recipe for spiritual and emotional disaster was remedied when Doug gave in to his father-in-law's urging to take up hunting. The woods and fields became a place of solitude for him. "Lord, it's just You and me out here," Doug said one day while hunting. "I'm listening; You speak to me." More than once Doug found those moments of solitude and silence to be a time of spiritual renewal where he could hear God and re-center his life and priorities around Christ.

As believers we feel the tension between doing lots of good things and spending time alone with God. Our spiritual journey is not a boot camp obstacle course where we vie to complete a series of rigorous tasks and reach the finish line first. It's more like a mountain climb where pulling aside to be reoriented and refreshed is not only beneficial, but also essential for our well-being. The spiritual practice of solitude and silence is a gift from God that gives us permission to pull aside from the noise and demands of daily life, take a deep breath, and receive fresh strength and direction for our journey.

THE PRIORITY OF SOLITUDE AND SILENCE

The passages of Scripture beginning with Mark 1:21 describe a day in the life of Jesus that would leave any of us needing to take a deep breath. After a day filled with teaching in the synagogue, exorcising an unclean spirit, and healing Simon Peter's mother-in-law, Jesus deserved a rest. But as soon as the sun set and Sabbath ended the whole town of Capernaum gathered at Simon's house for Jesus to heal the sick and drive out demons. From early morning to late evening Jesus met people in need, restored their lives, and demonstrated the authority of the kingdom of God. Yet Jesus seems to have found something distressing about what took place during that day; something that needed to be sorted out in His own mind and spirit.

Read Mark 1:35-39 below. What steps did Jesus take to work through His concerns?

> 35 *Very early in the morning, while it was still dark, He got up,*
> *went out, and made His way to a deserted place. And He was*
> *praying there.* 36 *Simon and his companions went searching for*
> *Him.* 37 *They found Him and said, "Everyone's looking for You!"*
> 38 *And He said to them, "Let's go on to the neighboring villages so*
> *that I may preach there too. This is why I have come."* 39 *So He*
> *went into all of Galilee, preaching in their synagogues and driving out demons.*

What concerned Jesus was a matter that could only be worked through in deep communion with His Father. **Very early the next morning**, sometime between 3 and 6 a.m., Jesus with great resolve and intentionality **got up, went out, and made His way** to a solitary place isolated from demands and interruptions. The only voice that could be heard was His own as He lifted up prayer toward the face of God. "Mark's portrait of Jesus is of a man busy and unable by day to escape the long and tiring demands of people in need. Victorious over Satan and his minions, healing every kind of disease, Jesus was nevertheless a man in need of prayer."[1]

Solitude and silence was a habit rather than a one-time occurrence for Jesus. Luke 5:16 tells us Jesus "often withdrew to deserted places and prayed."

Read the Bible passages below and list reasons Jesus may have withdrawn to pray in each instance.

Matthew 14:6-13

Mark 14:32-36

Luke 6:12-13

John 6:4-15

At critical moments in Jesus' ministry the most important thing He could do was spend time alone with God. Only then could all things be put in perspective. Other priorities could only be clearly determined once the ultimate priority of time alone with God was in place. It was in times of solitude and silence that Jesus reaffirmed His mission and was refreshed to remain on His journey until the victorious end.

Imagine, if you will, a possible scene at Simon's house that morning. People in need of healing, as well as curious onlookers, may have returned looking for Jesus. But He wasn't there and no one knew where He was. Simon, who often saw the need to act on Jesus' behalf as if the Lord couldn't take care of Himself, may have been concerned Jesus was missing an opportunity to build on His success and popularity. He and **his companions** (v. 36) went on an intense search to track Him down and bring Him back to the crowd that had gathered. When **they found Him** they described the situation succinctly, "**Everyone's looking for You!**" The needs—or at least the desires—of the people were clearly evident and the opportunity was right. In their opinion Jesus needed to seize the moment, not allow it to slip away.

Jesus did seize the moment, not to build His popularity, but to teach His misguided but well-intentioned followers that He would not be the possession of any one group, nor was His mission localized or institutionalized. He had not come to be the town doctor but the world's Savior. During His period of solitude Jesus heard the voice of His Father reaffirming who He was, why He was on earth, and what His next steps would be. That voice rising above the clamor of people demanding His attention determined His priorities.

What sets the framework for the priorities in your life—the expectations of others or an agenda that comes from having spent time with God?

Certainly as Jesus spent time in solitude and silence His Father assured Him what He had accomplished in Capernaum was good, but He must be about the best. He was empowered to stay focused on fulfilling His Father's mission even though it meant personal sacrifice. He invited others to join Him. The phrase **Let's go** (v. 38), which can be rendered "Let's be going, and keep on going," emphasizes the ongoing nature of His mission.

How might the spiritual practice of solitude and silence help you "keep on going" in your journey toward Christlikeness?

Jesus' determined practice of time alone with God enabled the whole of His ministry and set all that He did in the context of the Father's will. In his commentary on the *Book of Mark*, Richard Glover provides an excellent perspective on Jesus' need for solitude and silence. "He wanted a greater heart than man's to rest on with his sorrows, cares, and toils, and He found it in the heart of God. He, as man, had to seek guidance for each day's action, and light for each day's teaching and power for each day's work; and only God could give these. And so, to Him . . . the altar of God was the nest of His soul."[2]

Refreshed by communion with the Father and having clarified the direction of His mission and ministry, Jesus **went into all of Galilee**. In verse 35 Jesus "went out" to pray; in verse 39 He went out to preach. Traveling from place to place He could be found **preaching in their synagogues**, proclaiming the good news in settings where people were assembled and open to hearing His message. Furthermore, He was engaged in **driving out demons**, giving evidence of the truth of His proclamation and demonstrating that within Him could be found a power and authority that exceeded all others.

Being a faithful disciple of Jesus Christ means to learn from Him by listening to Him and following His example. Much can be said in favor of the contemplative lifestyle. But as Jesus has modeled for us, being contemplative is not the end. We contemplate the things of God so that we might be prepared to act according to His calling, will, and purpose. Those who listen attentively and act faithfully will also enjoy the blessing of victory.

THE PRIVILEGE OF SOLITUDE AND SILENCE

Unlike Jesus, many people are afraid of being alone and silent. Why is that?

What about you—do you crave or fear solitude and silence and why?

The memory verse for this study is Psalm 46:10 which reads in the *Holman Christian Standard Bible*, "Stop your fighting—and know that I am God." You perhaps have heard this verse in a version that says, "Be still and know I am God" (KJV and NIV). These differing translations are complementary, for we so often fight being still. Have you ever tried to hold down a wiggling, fighting toddler? The little tyke acts like you are imposing on him the worst kind of torture when all you want to do is clean his face, pull out a splinter, or simply love on him for a minute. We adults can act just like that squirming toddler, fearfully avoiding solitude and silence as if it were some kind of torture. Meanwhile God urges us to stop fighting and be still so He can cleanse us, heal us, or simply love on us. Solitude and silence is not some kind of painful penance; it's a great privilege with many benefits.

Solitude removes us from the distraction of people and activities into a more concentrated awareness of God's presence. By coming before Him in silence, speaking and other outward stimuli are negated and we are able to be more focused on what God wants us to hear and learn from Him.

Angela, like many 20-somethings, was really struggling to discern God's plan for her life. After exploring options, fretting, and soliciting others' advice she determined to get away for a day and seek God's direction. Armed with a Bible and playlist of worship songs, she sat on the bank of a lake, prepared to receive a great revelation about where to go and what to do. Instead, she said, "God wouldn't let me ask Him what I was supposed to do. He just kept telling me, 'Seek Me, seek Me.'" For hours she listened to the same song and read the same Bible passage over and over again. When she left the lake she still didn't have clear direction but she had an all-consuming peace and certainty that God loved her, was in control, and would tell her what to do when she needed to do it. That time of solitude and silence gave her what she really needed, greater intimacy with God, which empowered her to confidently take the next steps on her life's journey.

Describe a time in your life when, as a result of a special period of communion with the Lord, you found clarity of life direction, acted on it, and received a blessing.

The practice of solitude and silence puts you in a posture to hear from God so He can transform you into the image of His Son. When you regularly choose to be alone and silent with God you will find yourself less and less under the influence of yourself and others and more under the influence of Christ. Becoming more like Jesus will give you divine wisdom to know when to speak and when to remain silent.

When you become more like Jesus through the spiritual practice of solitude and silence you will become more compassionate, able to sense others' needs and willing to serve them gladly. You will become a gentler, calmer, and deeper person as you discipline yourself to be still, quiet, and reflective on the things of God. You will be controlled by God rather than the "tyranny of the urgent" as you determine and live by God's good priorities for your life.

The spiritual practice of solitude and silence can instill in you the discipline to let God be the Judge and Justifier. When you trust God to work things out and deal with people instead of thinking you've got to jump in and handle it all immediately you will enjoy greater emotional and physical health. When you are alone in the presence of God you don't have to do anything or be like anyone else to be accepted. You can stop fighting to earn God's pleasure. You can stop fighting to fix everything and everybody. You can simply be yourself and be still, knowing God accepts you based on who you are in Christ, not on anything you do.

What benefits would you love to gain by practicing solitude and silence?

THE PRACTICE OF SOLITUDE AND SILENCE

Jesus invites all His followers to, "Come away by yourselves to a remote place and rest for a while" (Mark 6:31). Just as Jesus took intentional steps to get up, go out, and make His way to a deserted place to pray, we also must take intentional steps to accept His invitation to experience solitude and silence and its many benefits.

One way to practice this spiritual discipline daily is to determine a time and place that belongs to you and God. Choose a place that becomes your haven of solitude and silence, a place that separates you from the demands and distractions that are part of your normal day. If you can't focus when your body is still, use your daily walk or run to be the place where you focus on listening to God.

In a perfect world nothing would interfere with your determination to be alone and silent for a few minutes every day. But the fact is, things will come up, chaos will ensue, and you will desperately need to "come away" with God and "rest for a while." Take advantage of daily opportunities for solitude. Turn off the morning news and enjoy your first cup of coffee with God. Take the stairs rather than the elevator and snatch those few steps to center yourself in God and His plans. Sit in a park at lunchtime silently communing with God as you focus on His creative handiwork. Step outside at night and focus on the God who created the stars and knows them by name (Ps. 147:4).

The location of your physical body is important to the practice of solitude and silence but not nearly as crucial as the condition of your heart. On the one hand, you can be alone and still not experience solitude while, on the other hand, you can be the middle of a crowd and enjoy solitude with God. You can sit in complete silence and not listen to God but hear Him clearly while in the midst of an uproar. The key is active silence where you intentionally focus on listening to God. To be still you must stop fighting God but never stop fighting inner and outer distractions that prevent you from being still and focusing on hearing and knowing Him.

What are some distractions you need to put away to practice solitude and silence?

Intentionally choosing to pull away to spend time in silence with God means intentionally turning off all technology. If music helps you focus on God, turn it on. If it distracts you, turn it off. If you are constantly bombarded by thoughts and to-do lists, jot them down and return to communing with God.

In addition to the benefit of daily opportunities for small moments of solitude, this practice calls for emulating Jesus and intentionally getting away to be with God. Attempt an extended period of time (around two hours or so) where you get alone and silent in order to decompress and begin to hear from God. This is an excellent opportunity to engage in the spiritual practice of journaling to reflect on and record what God is teaching and revealing to you in the silence. If an hour or two seems daunting to you, start with 30 minutes; God's not looking at the clock, just your heart.

The deeper you immerse into this practice the more you'll want to spend longer periods of solitude and silence with the Lord. Work up to where you spend an entire day alone with God in special seasons of retreat at a lake, the mountains, or retreat center. Listen to God through reading and meditating on His Word, observing Him in the surroundings, and paying attention to the still small voice of His Spirit speaking within. Consider making it a regular practice to pull aside a few days a year to be refreshed and rediscover "Who am I? Why am I here? Where am I? What are my next steps on this journey?" In this world of constant noise, solitude and silence is a gift from God that you should readily accept.

Set a timer for 15 minutes. Then sit in silence, actively listening to God. Record what He says in the space provided below. Try 20 minutes tomorrow and 30 minutes next week.

[1] Henry E. Turlington, "Mark" in *General Articles, Matthew-Mark, The Broadman Bible Commentary*, vol. 8 (Nashville: Broadman Press, 1969), 276.

[2] Richard Glover, A *Teacher's Commentary on the Gospel of St. Mark* (London: Marshall, Morgan and Scott, 1957), 19.

CHAPTER 3

SUFFERING AND PERSEVERANCE

WHY, AND TO WHAT PURPOSE?

WHY STUDY THIS LESSON? The Bible teaches perseverance is something we develop through trials and sufferings of life, and God uses these times to bring about our spiritual maturity.

BACKGROUND PASSAGE	FOCAL PASSAGE	MEMORY VERSES
ROMANS 5:1-11	ROMANS 5:1-5	ROMANS 5:3-4

BITTER OR BETTER

Sherry was a loyal and exemplary employee. She had worked hard to reach the position she had attained with her company. The quality of her work was superior and her coworkers admired her. Then late Friday afternoon she was called to her supervisor's office. Her irritation at a last-minute meeting before the weekend was overtaken by devastation when she discovered she was being let go. In the privacy of her car on the way home, she wept bitterly. How could such a thing happen to her? She didn't deserve it.

As Sherry struggled with how to deal with the unfair hand dealt to her, she thought about her friend Dana who had suffered through chemotherapy, a mastectomy, and bone marrow transplant. Although her cancer went into remission, radiation treatments had damaged Dana's lungs so badly that she eventually had a double lung transplant. Sherry watched Dana persevere through all her suffering with dignity. When she asked Dana her secret, this Christ-centered believer answered, "I just decided giving up on life and faith was simply not an option for me." As Sherry pondered Dana's struggle-filled, yet joyful, journey she realized she could not always choose what happened to her, but she could choose her response.

What are my options when it comes to responding to disappointments, hurts, or trials?

What might be the results of each choice?

Contrary to the claims of some popular (and false) preachers that God's faithful people always enjoy physical and financial prosperity, Jesus warned that those who follow Him will have suffering in this world (John 16:33). Christians are not to seek suffering, but we can seek to become better rather than bitter through our trials. Such a positive outcome occurs when we determine giving up is not an option and choose to allow God to use trials to teach us perseverance, train us in godliness, and transform us more into the image of His Son.

A BETTER WAY

In the first four chapters of Romans, Paul presented the theme of his letter: justification by faith. All people have sinned, causing them to be less than what God intended and making them subject to God's wrath. However, God provided a way of redemption, release, and relief through faith in Jesus Christ. In chapter five, Paul celebrated the benefits of choosing God's better way.

Underline benefits of being in Christ in Romans 5:1-5 below.

> 1 *Therefore, since we have been declared righteous by faith, we have peace with God through our Lord Jesus Christ.* 2 *We have*

also obtained access through Him by faith into this grace in which
we stand, and we rejoice in the hope of the glory of God. 3 *And not*
only that, but we also rejoice in our afflictions, because we know
that affliction produces endurance, 4 *endurance produces proven*
character, and proven character produces hope. 5 *This hope will*
not disappoint us, because God's love has been poured out in our
hearts through the Holy Spirit who was given to us.

LIVING IN GOD'S PEACE

Paul had previously asserted all that violates God's holy nature and purpose is subject to His just wrath and indignation (Rom. 1:18). But now **since we have been declared righteous**, or justified, **by faith**, we are relieved of that threat and live in **peace with God**. The word "justified" has its background in the world of law when a judge acquits a defendant and allows that person to walk away free. Believers are free from sin and in a right relationship with God because God declares us not guilty. **Faith** in **our Lord Jesus Christ** is responding to what God has made possible, believing to the point of trusting, and trusting to the point of acting on what we profess to believe and trust.

What does it mean to you to be in a right relationship with God?

How can you appropriately respond to God declaring you "not guilty"?

Peace with God is one of the benefits that come to the believer **through** (by means of) Christ. Usually, we think of peace to mean an absence of conflict. However, the word translated "peace" includes much more. It is a state of well-being in which we experience the fullness of a positive relationship with God and the assurance of knowing we have been accepted by Him. Even when adversity or suffering comes, the person who has peace with God is not threatened.

How can knowing you are at peace with God influence your attitude and responses during times of suffering or trial?

STANDING IN GOD'S GRACE

Another benefit believers receive is **this grace in which we stand** (v. 2). Is there any more beautiful word in Scripture than *grace*? We describe it as amazing, marvelous, and abundant. Grace is God's unmerited favor, goodwill, or loving-kindness toward us even when we are not deserving of it—which we never are. Our right standing before Him is a product of His grace, not a result of our personal effort or goodness. Grace is not limited to the salvation experience. We live daily by grace, with and in God's favor.

Stand can mean to be firmly established and immoveable; something firm and enduring. The believer's life is firmly established in God's divine favor. No opposition, circumstances, adversity, or suffering can remove us from that state of grace. We are able to stand firmly in the realm of grace because we **obtained access through Him by faith**. *Obtained* suggests we secured it from another. Think of it in terms of something you own. The object did not just appear out of nowhere. You got it from somewhere. That is the sense in this verse. We obtained access into divine grace and favor when we placed our faith in Jesus to forgive our sins and give us abundant life both now and forever.

Our response to receiving all these benefits is to **rejoice in the hope of the glory of God** (v. 2b). *Rejoice* can mean "boast." Since we cannot create peace with God or gain access to grace on our own, we have no cause to boast about ourselves. But we can boast about God. *Hope* in the biblical sense is not wishful thinking but confident expectation. It is not possibility, but certainty. We live in the assurance that God can be counted on to accomplish His will and Word. Such hope is rooted in, motivated by, and focused on the glory of God. *Glory* refers to the praise, honor, and worship that God is due by virtue of who He is.

What is one of your favorite songs about God's grace?

When times are tough how does that song, or any reminder of God's grace, encourage you to:

Stand firm in faith?

Boast in God and give Him glory?

Hang on to hope?

BELIEVING IN GOD'S ABILITY

Without the truths declared in Romans 5:1-2, verses 3-4 would be pure foolishness, unreasonable, and impossible. However, because they are true, we can **rejoice in our afflictions** (v. 3). What an unusual statement. Who rejoices or boasts about being in trouble?

Afflictions is a general term for any kind of trouble, distress, or pressures exerted on us, whether brought on by poor decisions by others, the outcome of living in a fallen world, or because of our commitment to live for Christ. No matter the cause of the affliction, the person of faith can rejoice. This does not mean we rejoice in the afflictions themselves but that we can find cause for joy in the midst of suffering. The peace, grace, and joy described in verses 1-2 are not destroyed or depleted by hard circumstances. We can rejoice because God is able to use the tough times for good to strengthen us and move us to be more like Christ.

To support his claim that believers can rejoice in afflictions, Paul strung together three virtues that God can bring to fruition through affliction. He asserts **we know** what he is about to say is so; it is not hearsay, a possibility, or a wish.

Look at Romans 5:3-4 in your Bible and identify those three virtues. Which virtue would you most rejoice to see in your life right now?

Affliction produces endurance. *Produces* is a verb that means to work out, achieve, or effect. Endurance is perseverance, a staying power that enables a person to be constant and steadfast. Without a doubt, the present reality, no matter how difficult, is not the final reality. We can actively confront problems to overcome them, rise above them, and grow through them. Afflictions may threaten to destroy us but we can endure by faith through Christ. That gives us reason to rejoice about what God has accomplished, is accomplishing, and will accomplish in us.

That is not all. **Endurance produces proven character**. *Proven character* denotes proof of authenticity as a result of having been tested. The word has a metallurgical background. Gold ore that is heated to such a degree that the impurities are skimmed away leaves pure gold. Those who endure the fiery test of trials develop and demonstrate integrity and authenticity of their commitment to Christ. The more we persevere in faith, the more we look like Jesus.

The final virtue in the trilogy is **hope**. Paul had already offered confidence in God as a cause for joy. Here *hope* is the reward that comes to the believer for persevering. Confidence in God grows the more hope is experienced. "There is a circularity in this. Hope makes it possible to endure, and at the same time the process of enduring and the godly character it produces increases our hope by making us continually reflect on the future realities guaranteed by God."[1]

How can we **know** this cycle of hope will occur when we persevere? We know it's true because we have seen it lived out in other people, because we have experienced it ourselves in the crucible of life, and because we can trust what God promises in His Word.

Reflect back on a time of personal affliction, pressure, or trouble. In what ways do you now see that God was at work developing Christ's character in you?

How does that memory give you hope to persevere during present struggles?

CLAIMING GOD'S HOPE

The person who lives according to a false promise is doomed to fail. Confidence built on a false promise is foolishness. How can a person depend on that which is not dependable? Such is not the case with hope in God. **This hope will not disappoint us** (v.5). *Disappoint* means to dishonor, disgrace, or make ashamed. You are not taking any risk when you claim God's hope.

The reliability of any promise is dependent on the credibility of the one making the promise. We can have confidence in God in trials because God is credible, His character impeccable, His integrity pure, and His ability unmatched. God is **love**. This divine attribute is not something God possesses; it is the essence of who He is. So all He does is an expression of His love. He cannot be unloving since that would be a denial of who He is. Paul used the word "agape," the term used most often in Scripture to describe God's kind of unconditional, sacrificial love. The *hope* we have in God will not, cannot, disappoint us because He loves us with an unparalleled, incomparable, and unending love.

His love isn't dispensed sparingly but lavished on us. **Poured out** suggests the imagery of the overflow that would occur by pouring water from a gallon bucket into a six-ounce teacup. The verb tense for **has been poured out** describes something that happened in the past with an effect that continues in the future. God's love toward us is not a onetime event nor does He have to refill His reservoir of love to give us more love. When our hearts are breaking and our journey seems too dark and painful to bear we can sing confidently to God, "Your love never fails, It never gives up, Never runs out on me."[2]

God's lavish outpouring of love is **through the Holy Spirit**. The Holy Spirit enters the life of the believer at conversion and makes available all that God has for us in Christ. We come to know and experience the love of God continually—even during hard times—through the abiding presence of His Holy Spirit. Because He loves us, we have hope. Our response is to reach out and claim it.

What can you do to reach out and claim God's hope when you are striving to faithfully persevere through struggles and heartache?

CHOOSING THE BETTER WAY

Compare Romans 5:1-5 with James 1:2-4. What similar truths are stated?

Can something good come from suffering? Yes it can, by living in God's peace, standing in His grace, believing He is able, and making a claim on the hope He lovingly makes available by faith in Christ. All of this doesn't happen automatically. You must intentionally choose the better way. Incorporating the spiritual practice of perseverance in your life means daily choosing to trust God and submit to His work in using trials to develop and prove Christ-like character and spiritual maturity in you. Consider the following suggestions for choosing the better way and allowing trials to mature you and make you complete in Christ.

CHOOSE A BETTER PERSPECTIVE

When a trial comes, put it in perspective. Identify factors contributing to the affliction. If it resulted from your poor choice, confess where necessary, make personal corrections, accept the consequences, and ask for God's strength to endure. If your trial is the result of someone else's poor decision, offer forgiveness as appropriate, and ask God to help you to become better through it rather than bitter toward the perpetrator or even God. If your life challenge is simply the result of living in a fallen world, ask the Lord for grace to trust Him through it even though you do not understand why it has befallen you. Then, as a sacrifice of praise, rejoice in the affliction because you know God is using it to produce a character in you that resembles His Son.

CHOOSE BETTER EXAMPLES

It is obvious from both Scripture and life that who we associate with greatly influences our attitudes and actions. Although you can't always avoid people who have chosen to become bitter through life's trials, you can be careful to not let their way of dealing with suffering become your way. Just as Sherry did with Dana, look to and learn from others who have endured in faith through trials and come out stronger.

The Bible is full of examples of people who endured suffering and experienced its redemptive powers. When Job begged God for an explanation for his suffering, he didn't get the answer he was looking for; instead, he got something better and more enduring. He came to know the vastness of God and His sovereign purpose. Job persevered, and eventually God brought great blessing into his life. The apostle Paul is another example of difficult things happening to good people. Paul was convinced that by persevering in faith he could claim victory, bring God glory, and grow to become more like Christ. Read 2 Corinthians to see more on his perspective on suffering and the glory that comes to those who endure in Christ.

CHOOSE A BETTER OUTLOOK

We don't always face great sufferings like Job, Paul, or Dana did, nor do we need to look for ways to suffer. Trials find us every day as we struggle to battle temptations, to not give up praying for something we've prayed for a long time, and to continue loving and serving even when we see no fruits of our labors. Choose to practice perseverance by facing all trials with dignity and with the positive outlook that God is with you, loves you, and is up to something good in your life. When troubles come, endure with steadfast patience, unwavering trust, and in the joy of being counted worthy to suffer for His Kingdom. Don't just endure with gritted teeth; endure with the expectation that God is at work in all things, even the bad things, to accomplish His purposes, which includes conforming you to the image of His Son. "Wait *and* hope for *and* expect the Lord; be brave *and* of good courage and let your heart be stout *and* enduring. Yes, wait for *and* hope for *and* expect the Lord" (Ps. 27:14, AMP).

Think about a specific trial or affliction you are experiencing now. Record the specifics of that trial in your journal, considering questions such as:

What is the best perspective about this trial and what steps is that perspective calling me to take?

Think of someone who has been an example for you of persevering through suffering. How has that person encouraged you to persevere in faith?

How can I have a better outlook about this time of affliction?

How will I face my trials with dignity so that I become better rather than bitter?

---

[1] Grant R. Osborne, Grant R Osborne, Series Editor, "Romans" in *The IVP New Testament Commentary Series*, vol. 6 (Downers Grove, IL: InterVarsity Press, 2004), 130-31.

[2] Brian Johnson, Christa Black-Gifford, Jeremy Riddle, *One Thing Remains (Your Love Never Fails)*, Bethel Music, 2010. http://www.worshipsong.com/songs/songdetails/one-thing-remains-your-love-never-fails

CHAPTER 4

GIFTS AND TALENTS

GIVEN FOR A PURPOSE

WHY STUDY THIS LESSON? Every believer has been given spiritual gifts and talents, to produce what is beneficial for God's people and God's work in the world.

BACKGROUND PASSAGE	FOCAL PASSAGE	MEMORY VERSE
1 CORINTHIANS 12	1 CORINTHIANS 12:4-11	1 PETER 4:10

GET ON THE SAME LEVEL

The world tends to elevate individuals to a level of importance because of some skill they possess. That guy is important because he has the highest scoring average on the basketball team. She is important because she is the most astute investor in the company. He is important because he is the smartest student in the class. Even in the church we may determine the best speaker on staff, worship team member with the most pleasing voice, or small-group participant with the deepest insight is on some higher level of importance than everyone else.

The journey toward a Christ-centered life is not traveled on a multi-decked highway with the greatest skilled believers on the top level and the lesser skilled on lower levels. In God's Kingdom every believer has value and skills essential to the proper functioning of the entire community of faith.

Stewardship is the purposeful responsible management of resources God has put into our care. The spiritual practice of stewardship of gifts and talents means we don't neglect our God-given abilities or use them to promote ourselves to a perceived higher level of importance. Rather, as we journey toward Christlikeness on the same level path with other believers, we intentionally focus on using the gifts God has entrusted to us to produce what's beneficial for God's people and His work in the world.

BE LEVELHEADED

Paul wrote First Corinthians to the believers in Corinth, a major city in Greece. The believers had been a united God-honoring body but in time succumbed to impure practices and became driven more by personal wants than godly desires. One area of church contention centered on the gifts of the Spirit. Some believers began to think of spiritual gifts more as status symbols than endowments for service and considered themselves to be more important than others because they possessed what they deemed to be the most important spiritual gifts.

Paul devoted chapters 12-14 of his letter to address this issue and urged believers to be levelheaded about spiritual gifts rather than using them to determine levels of importance.

Based on 1 Corinthians 12:4-11 below, how can believers be levelheaded about the differences in abilities that exist in the church?

> *4 Now there are different gifts, but the same Spirit. 5 There are*
> *different ministries, but the same Lord. 6 And there are different*
> *activities, but the same God activates each gift in each person. 7*
> *A demonstration of the Spirit is given to each person to produce*
> *what is beneficial: 8 to one is given a message of wisdom through*
> *the Spirit, to another, a message of knowledge by the same Spirit,*
> *9 to another, faith by the same Spirit, to another, gifts of healing*

by the one Spirit, 10 to another, the performing of miracles, to another, prophecy, to another, distinguishing between spirits, to another, different kinds of languages , to another, interpretation of languages. 11 But one and the same Spirit is active in all these, distributing to each person as He wills.

DIFFERENT GIFTS, SAME SOURCE

We can be levelheaded when we realize different doesn't mean more or less important; it simply means different. You surely see in your own fellowship people with different abilities involved in different **ministries** and **activities** (vv. 5-6). The differences are not to categorize people into levels of importance but to reflect the essential unity of their common source of **the same Spirit** . . . **the same Lord** . . . **the same God**, which we recognize as the three persons of the Godhead. "All spiritual gifts come from God the Father, who was made known through His Son Jesus Christ and indwells every believer through His Holy Spirit."[1] Therefore, every gift, ministry, and activity is to point to God, the source and power who **activates each gift in each person**.

DIFFERENT GIFTS, COMMON GOOD

We can be levelheaded about gifts we have and don't have when we recognize the reason God gives believers different gifts and abilities. Verse 7 is packed with insight critical to being a good steward of our gifts and talents.

First, a **demonstration**, meaning "a manifestation, expression, or bestowment," **of the Spirit is given**. Some Bible teachers distinguish between spiritual gifts as miraculous abilities given a person for use in particular situations and the natural talents and abilities cultivated from one's interests. We shall take the more comprehensive view that says everything that makes us who we are—our natural talents, interests, cultivated abilities, along with any special manifestations—are blessings given by God through the indwelling of the Holy Spirit. Blessings, no matter what form they take, are by nature demonstrations of God's favor.

What are some demonstrations of the Spirit you think you have been given? Why did these come to mind?

Second, the giving of these manifestations of the Spirit is all-inclusive; something **is given to each person**. Contrary to what we might think about some people or even ourselves, no one is left out. Everyone in the family of God is a recipient of at least one demonstration of His grace. Some people have more than one but no one has all of them. Therefore, every member of the body is important to the functioning of the whole; every member has something to contribute and every person has some dependence on others.

Some people refuse opportunities to work in some ministry by saying they are not capable of doing anything or have no spiritual gifts. How does verse 7 prove that to be incorrect and inappropriate?

We may think a person who responds in the way described above is doing so from a sense of personal humility. Dr. J. W. MacGorman challenges such thinking, "The person who depreciates himself as being unable to do anything significant for the Lord is not humble. Rather he is undiscerning and perhaps ungrateful."[2]

Gratitude is a major factor in being levelheaded about spiritual gifts. Think about a really nice gift a loved one has given you. Do you keep it in the box and declare you are unworthy to use that item? Do you feel arrogant about possessing that gift or gratitude for that person's generosity toward you? God has graced you with at least one spiritual gift. You are a good steward when you take intentional steps to determine what that gift is and then humbly and gratefully use it to serve God and others.

The manifestations of the Spirit given to each believer are given **to produce what is beneficial**. Whenever and however we are gifted, we are to use our blessing to be a blessing to others. Our spiritual gifts are not for our own benefit; neither are they spiritual merit badges we wear to call attention to ourselves. The gifts, talents, and abilities we have are not exclusively ours; they belong to the community of believers. If they are not being used for the benefit of others, then our gifts and talents are being misused and the congregation is being cheated.

Look back at the demonstrations of the Spirit you have been given. How are you using each to benefit others?

Paul listed nine demonstrations of the Spirit given to members of the church in Corinth (vv. 8-10). The list is not all-inclusive, but representative. Other lists can be found in 1 Corinthians 12:28, Romans 12:6-8, Ephesians 4:11-12 and 1 Peter 4:10-11. You may want to read and compare those lists. Even then, we are not to conclude these lists are all-inclusive even when combined.

Paul provided virtually no explanation about the gifts he listed, so we must assume the Corinthian readers understood the list against the backdrop of what was taking place in the church there. Because we are so far removed by time and culture from Corinth, consider the following brief comments to gain some understanding of what each gift was and the purpose it served.

- **A message of wisdom:** Wisdom as a spiritual gift is more than being smart or having the ability to make good decisions. It is a special ability derived from spiritual insight to discern and apply knowledge and practices essential for godly living.
- **A message of knowledge:** The spiritual gift of knowledge goes beyond possessing information about the Christian message and way of life. It is spiritual knowledge that understands what renews the mind and transforms the heart; the whole person.
- **Faith:** All believers have saving faith, which itself is a gift from God. Faith in this setting likely refers to deep convictions in the ability of God to do mighty things.
- **Gifts of healing:** Supernatural healing of the sick was part of Jesus' ministry and the work of the early church. The healings bore witness to the authority of Christ, illustrated the

spiritual change He came to bring in a person's life, and were a foretaste of the complete life to come in heaven.

- **Performing of miracles:** This is a reference to other miraculous occurrences that come through the Spirit. Miracles provided authentication of the Christian message in the early days of the church.
- **Prophecy:** Throughout Scripture prophecy can be understood as *forth-telling*, declaring a message for the moment under direct inspiration from the Lord; and as *fore-telling*, an insight into and knowledge of the future. Either way it is a message from the Lord intended to lead people to a confessional response and to anticipate something God is about to do.
- **Distinguishing between spirits:** Some understand this gift to be the ability to perceive the difference between demonic spirits and the Spirit of the Lord. Others see it as the ability to distinguish between false and true teachers.
- **Different kinds of languages:** The interpretations of this gift vary and create some degree of controversy among contemporary Christians just as it did in first century Corinth. Whatever the form—different languages, ecstatic utterances, or something else—Paul acknowledged them as a gift given by the Spirit. The problem in Corinth was that this gift had become a status symbol rather than a gift that served the church and contributed to congregational unity.
- **Interpretation of languages:** This gift is the ability to interpret human language or the deep spiritual longings expressed as otherwise unintelligible utterance, so the whole body can be built up and encouraged by understanding what was being said.

These gifts had particular meaning to the Corinthian church's ministry and had been misunderstood or misrepresented, leading to the conflict Paul was addressing. One gift should not be seen as more important than another. As someone noted, God uses both the blinding brightness of the sun and the twinkling of the stars to bring light into His world. Rather than feeling inadequate to those people who seem to shine with many talents and abilities, we can consider how we and those especially gifted believers can complement one another in serving the Lord.

DIFFERENT GIFTS, SAME GRACE

Paul repeated the single source for all spiritual gifts and talents since that clearly was something the Corinthians needed to hear. The energy to work and the effectiveness of the work accomplished through us are dependent on the Holy Spirit. Paul also reemphasized that the Spirit distributes gifts **to each person as He wills** (v. 11), according to His plan and purpose. The giving of manifestations of the Spirit is a sovereign act of God. He gives them by His grace, meaning according to His favor. No one earns them or deserves them, so no one has any reason to boast about gifts, talents, or abilities. If you believe that what God does, He does with purpose and according to His standard of what is right, then you should not feel inferior if you have fewer gifts than someone else.

Just as the gifts you have are because of God's grace and favor; so too are the gifts you don't have. So don't get the big head about gifts you have or the small head about gifts you lack. Be levelheaded about the unique gifts and abilities God has given you and use them with gratitude to fulfill God's purposes for your life in His kingdom.

According to 1 Peter 4:10-11, what are God's purposes for the gifts He's given you?

Look again at the gifts and abilities you listed earlier. List at least two below and beside each one note how you are being a good steward of that gift and how God is being glorified as a result.

A LEVELHEADED EXAMPLE

Paul left his young protégé Timothy in Ephesus to lead the church while he attended to ministry elsewhere. To support Timothy during his absence, Paul wrote him a letter of encouragement and advice. In 1 Timothy 4:13, he counseled Timothy to give attention to public reading of the Scripture, exhort others to obey its message, and teach them how to apply it to living.

According to 1 Timothy 4:14, how could Paul have such confidence in Timothy and how could Timothy have confidence in himself?

The assignment was not just from Paul and its fulfillment was not dependent on Timothy's personal ability alone. God had called and equipped Timothy to serve. That calling was affirmed by church leaders who recognized the gifts God had given him for ministry. Timothy's effectiveness in service was rooted in three truths that have implications for contemporary believers:

1. God had called him to service. *Indeed, the Lord has a place of service for everyone.*
2. God had gifted him. *The Lord equips us for whatever assignment He gives us.*
3. Timothy proved to be a faithful steward of the opportunities and gifts the Lord provided. *We too are challenged to be good stewards of the opportunities, gifts, talents, and abilities the Lord gives us to benefit God's people and His work in the world.*

TAKE IT TO THE NEXT LEVEL

As with every spiritual practice, you must move beyond the level of learning about the stewardship of gifts and talents and begin to apply yourself to discover what those gifts are and put them to work. Some misconceptions may need to be cleared away to have the proper desire and motivation for being a good steward of the gifts and talents God has given you.

Some people mistakenly think they aren't serving God unless they're miserably doing something they hate to do. Usually what God calls us to do is what we like to do because He has planted that passion and ability within us. There are few things more gratifying than doing what you love to do, are gifted at doing, and positively influencing people in the process. Every believer has been given a spiritual gift to serve the church. You are not to neglect or misuse them for selfish purposes, but rather, use them for the common good of God's people and his work. That's for your good and His glory.

We can learn from the Corinthians' negative example that we must be extremely careful of pride and legalism when it comes to spiritual gifts. The goal of this spiritual practice is not to check off "used my gifts" on the good Christian list to impress God and others. The goal is to put us into a posture to hear from God and allow Him to move us further along toward becoming like Jesus.

How could discovering and using your spiritual gifts and talents put you into a position to hear from God so He can conform you into the image of Christ?

When you discover your gifts, passions, and talents you can plug your unique personality and abilities into ministries, inside and outside the church, that maximize your impact in God's kingdom and give you the greatest joy in serving. Below are some simple suggestions for implementing the spiritual practice of the stewardship of spiritual gifts and talents.

Spiritual practices don't happen by default but by determination. Star each suggestion you will intentionally choose to take. Check off each suggestion after you have taken that action.

- Identify your spiritual gifts by taking a spiritual gifts inventory assessment.
- List your talents and explore ways they could be used in existing ministries in your church. Talking with church leaders can help discover areas in which your gifts and abilities can be activated.
- List areas of personal interest. Determine ways these interests could lead to beginning a new ministry.
- You may not realize you like and are gifted to do something unless you try it. So be willing to try ministries inside and

outside the church. If it fits you, keep at it. If it doesn't, keep trying out new ways to use your gifts to serve.

- Talk with a trusted friend or advisor who will help you do an honest assessment of your spiritual gifts, talents, and abilities.
- Ask the Lord to reveal to you how you can serve Him best out of your own giftedness.
- Thank the Lord for the ways and opportunities He has given you to serve.
- Commit to being a faithful steward of all you are, what you have, and your spiritual gifts, talents, and abilities.
- Periodically review how you've been investing the gifts and talents God has given you.

Write a prayer to thank God for what He has given you; commit afresh each gift to His service; and ask Him for additional opportunities to serve Him with the gifts and talents He has entrusted to you.

---

[1] Bob Reccord, *Helping Your Church Stay on Course: Studies in 1 Corinthians*, Adult Learner Guide, January Bible Study 2003 (Nashville: LifeWay Press, 2002), 66.

[2] J. W. MacGorman, *The Gifts of the Spirit: An Exposition of 1 Corinthians 12-14* (Nashville: Broadman Press, 1974), 31.

CHAPTER 5

GODLY COUNSEL

THE WISE SEEKER

WHY STUDY THIS LESSON? God has provided the Scriptures as our primary means of understanding His will, but He also provides a community of faith to help discern how He is at work and to assist in making God-honoring decisions.

BACKGROUND PASSAGE	FOCAL PASSAGE	MEMORY VERSE
ACTS 11:19-30; ACTS 13	ACTS 13:1-3	PROVERBS 11:14

SEEKING GUIDANCE

Candace, a married mother of two, considered returning to college but wondered if that was wise because of responsibilities at home. In what seemed coincidental but proved to be providential, she met Stella, a community professional, at a women's event at her church. Candace learned Stella's story had been much like hers. Godly counsel from Stella convinced Candace that returning to school was part of God's plan for her life.

The pastor and deacons at Faith Church believed the Lord was leading them to expand their ministry in new ways in the community. They called the congregation together and shared their vision. Rather than asking the members to vote on the matter, they led them to worship the Lord, humble themselves before Him, and pray for a revelation from Him. In time, the Lord spoke clearly and powerfully. The congregation was certain they were to move forward in ministry expansion just as their spiritual leaders had counseled them to do.

As Christians, we encounter many crossroads on this spiritual journey called life and aren't always sure which way to turn. To move further along toward a Christ-centered life we must make decisions that honor the Lord and benefit others. Certainly God guides individual Christians through His Scriptures and Spirit, but He has also given us the wonderful gift of a community of believers to help us discern His will and guide us on our journey. It is to our great benefit to seek godly counsel as we seek answers to life's questions: Who am I? Why am I here? Where am I? What are my next steps?

Check which statement describes how you usually make big decisions.

__ On my own. **__With the guidance of others.**

When I think about seeking godly counsel I feel:

Resistant because

Receptive because

SEEKING GOD'S WILL

The Book of Acts sets the apostle Paul's ministry in the context of three missionary journeys. His home base was Antioch of Syria where the believers possessed a strong missionary spirit and determination to burst beyond traditions that sometimes hindered the church in Jerusalem. Because Antioch was an international commercial center, the population was diverse. Hence, the church at Antioch had a more open view of the world and understood the gospel was for all people not just some people or "our" people.

According to Acts 13:1-3 below, what did that understanding lead the church to do?

1 In the church that was at Antioch there were prophets and
teachers: Barnabas, Simeon who was called Niger, Lucius the
Cyrenian, Manaen, a close friend of Herod the tetrarch, and Saul.
2 As they were ministering to the Lord and fasting, the Holy Spirit
said, "Set apart for Me Barnabas and Saul for the work I have
called them to." 3 Then after they had fasted, prayed, and laid
hands on them, they sent them off.

GODLY COUNSEL AND SPIRITUAL LEADERS

The active presence of effective leaders is essential to any organization. Effective leaders are marked by competency, integrity, sincerity, reliability, and insight. Of course, they need to know how to lead others and where they are leading them. They need to have a vision, understand the mission, and be able to communicate both to those whom they lead. Leaders with these qualities who are also filled with the Holy Spirit are no less needed in the church. While every individual is accountable and responsible to submit to the leadership of the Holy Spirit, as an organization a church still needs those who lead and influence.

What qualities do you admire about your pastor and/or other leaders in your church?

Pray for that person, thanking God for his or her leadership and asking for His blessing on the person. Consider sending a note or email expressing appreciation for his or her leadership.

The church at Antioch was blessed with such a leadership team of **prophets and teachers** (v. 1). We may understand these words to refer to official positions or they may indicate functions critical to the overall work of the church on mission in its setting. Those who were endowed with the gifts for carrying out those functions influenced the church and its ministry by training others in ministry and focusing on building up the body. Prophets in the Old Testament tradition received and declared a specific message from the Lord for a specific situation. Teachers were those with gifts for instructing others in God's truth as revealed in His Word. Teaching could have an evangelistic thrust focused on leading others to salvation or an emphasis designed to help believers understand the finer points of the Word and its relevance for Christian living. The most effective teachers do both.

Other than their names, we know little about these leaders except **Barnabas** and **Saul**. Members of the Jerusalem church gave a man named Joseph the nickname Barnabas, meaning "Son of Encouragement," because of his generosity and encouragement. Following Saul's conversion, Barnabas endorsed Saul when some questioned his sincerity in preaching the gospel (Acts 9:26-27).

Who in my community of faith is a Barnabas who stands with others to offer encouragement and counsel?

How can I be a Son or Daughter of Encouragement in my fellowship of believers?

Another leader was **Simeon**, nicknamed **Niger** meaning "black." He may have been from Africa along with **Lucius** from Cyrene, located on the north coast of Africa. An individual we might be surprised to see on a list of church leaders is **Manaen, a close friend of Herod** who reigned in Galilee during Jesus' ministry. Some think he was a foster brother to Herod. Whether friends or relatives, the two are an interesting contrast. As adults they were exposed to Jesus and given the same opportunity. Manaen became a follower of Christ and a Christian leader. Herod was so obsessed with his throne he had John the Baptist executed and refused Jesus the justice He deserved.

As surprised as we might be to see Manaen's name on the list of church leaders, many in Jerusalem would have been astounded to see Saul's name. This man's amazing transformation from persecutor of the church to preacher to the world is at the heart of Acts and attested to in the letters Paul wrote which make up the bulk of the New Testament.

Here we see a church under the influence of a group of diverse leaders gifted in the Lord, mature in the faith, and influential in the body.

Why is diversity among believers a great benefit in seeking and discerning God's will?

GODLY COUNSEL AND SEEKING THE LORD

The use of the pronoun **they** (v. 2) raises the question whether *they* are the five leaders or the assembly of believers at Antioch. Possibly what we see is a combination of the Holy Spirit identifying His choice for missionary service to the five and the church confirming the choice. As Paul would declare through his analogy of the church as a body, a church is strongest when every member is joined with others in service to the Lord. Even where the contributions of individuals are highlighted, the individuals were authorized and confirmed by the church.

Whether "they" refers to the five leaders or the entire church, it was in the context of **ministering to the Lord** and fasting that they received a revelation from the Holy Spirit. Ministering means "serving," but frequently the word was understood to mean "worshiping." That would not be foreign to us, for we sometimes speak of our worship gatherings as "worship services." We serve the Lord best when we bow before Him in worship, declaring His worth and submitting to His authority. Fasting, or abstinence from eating, suggests the church was earnestly seeking the Lord's direction and posturing itself for a revelation from Him. They had suspended all normal activity to focus attention on God. Submitting before the Lord in worship and focusing on the Lord by refraining from anything that would hinder one's spiritual hearing would create an environment in which the **Holy Spirit** could speak.

The church at Antioch had already shown its commitment to sharing the gospel (See Acts 11:19-26). The Lord had been doing a mighty work in their midst. The people had been influenced by the godly counsel that came in the form of prophetic messages and teaching by their leaders. As a result the church may have come to sense God had an expanded ministry for them of taking the gospel to unreached peoples beyond Antioch. They joined in intense worship and fasting to seek the Lord's guidance. In response to their earnest seeking, the Lord spoke through the Holy Spirit.

The Holy Spirit's directive was to **Set apart**, "to mark off from others, to appoint for some purpose," Barnabas and Saul. No reason was given for His choosing these two nor did He define what the **work** was. The Lord is not required to explain His choices, for He is sovereign. He knows best; He does best. The church, in obedience to the Holy Spirit, set apart the two men for the special work He had for them. The details of that work would continue to unfold as Barnabas and Saul obeyed Him in what they knew. We have a tendency to want to know beforehand the details of what the Lord is calling us to do. He does not always provide them, but wants us to be faithful to do what we know.

When was a time in your life you were convinced God had directed you to do something but He didn't supply all the details?

How did you discern the next steps you were to take?

What did you learn from that experience that you would do the same or differently the next time you face a decision?

The church did not see this mission as belonging exclusively to Barnabas and Saul. The church was on mission and willing to accept their responsibility for it. Thus they again **fasted** (v. 3); perhaps to affirm what had been revealed and declare their intentions to be faithful to it. They **prayed**, perhaps a prayer of thanksgiving for the revelation given to them, for the privilege of being able to share the gospel, for faithful leaders who offered godly counsel, and for safety for Barnabas and Saul during the travels on which they would soon embark. Then they **laid hands on them**, a sign of affirmation, confirmation, and solidarity. This was not an ordination to ministry that confirmed any rights, privileges, or authority, but an endorsement or a commissioning by fellow believers.

Then **they sent them off**, meaning "to set free, release, let go." The church acknowledged the will of God and the call of the Holy Spirit and gladly cooperated. Barnabas and Saul were released by the church from their current ministry assignment to a new ministry of which they all were a part. The two would return to share reports and renew fellowship for they always felt themselves under the authority of the congregation of believers at Antioch.

Acts 13:1-3 reflects the diversity of the church, its sense of mission, desire to expand its ministry, and responsiveness to the revelation of the Holy Spirit. Eagerly and earnestly, the church at Antioch endorsed the missionary ministry of Barnabas and Saul and released them to it. God continues to provide a community of faith to help us discern how He is at work and to assist us in making God-honoring decisions. We can receive godly counsel through conversation with others. We can also hear the "voice" of God and discern the will of God through the church gathered in worship and focused on hearing from Him.

SEEKING GODLY COUNSEL

Seeking godly counsel is a spiritual discipline every believer can practice. Consider the Stop, Look, and Listen approach as you strive to intentionally implement this practice in your life.

STOP

Stop racing to make decisions and stop being too proud to ask for guidance in making God-honoring decisions.

Why might some believers resist seeking godly counsel from others?

We need to stop being self-sufficient. Seeking godly counsel is not a sign of weakness but of strength and maturity. It requires humility, a teachable attitude, a submissive spirit, and a willingness to be accountable to others. Gaining spiritual guidance from others calls for a determination to stop our busyness and spend time seeking God's will with other believers through prayer, Bible study, and godly conversation.

LOOK

If you are not convinced seeking godly counsel is for you, invest a few minutes to look at the benefits of receiving godly counsel from mature believers.

What benefits might I gain in seeking godly counsel?

When it comes to seeking guidance from godly believers, you've got everything to gain and nothing to lose. You gain a deep friendship with a godly person who knows you well and values you anyway. You gain greater insight into discerning God's best and fulfilling His purpose for your life. You progress further toward Christlikeness and attain greater spiritual wisdom to provide godly counsel for others.

Godly counsel provides a different perspective and objectivity about decisions we're facing. We can be tempted to try to fit Scripture into our thinking and wishes. Counsel from objective mature believers helps us be true to Scripture and see where we're being self-centered rather than Christ-centered. Godly counsel helps us see the big picture so we don't get lost and lose hope in the immediate issues.

Absolutely crucial to the practice of godly counsel is looking for mature Spirit-led believers you trust to offer biblical counsel, earnest prayer, and spiritual guidance. Look for Christ-followers who have experienced what you are facing. Spend time with believers who have succeeded in areas where you want to succeed—who confidently share their faith, use their gifts and talents to benefit others, and live to serve others and honor Christ. Strive to be in close communication with believers who make it a daily practice to pray and be in God's Word and are intentional about their own journey toward Christ-likeness.

Be cautious of those who are quick to give answers and advice; instead look for counselors who ask questions and listen to really know you and the situation. Seek guidance from those who offer truth from God's Word rather than their own opinions. Don't look for people to tell you what you want to hear but, speaking the truth in love, tell you what you need to hear. Look for those sons or daughters of encouragement who won't just say, "You should do this," but "You can do this," by encouraging you to claim and live by Scripture and the power of the Holy Spirit.

This lesson's memory verse states, *Without guidance, people fall, but with many counselors there is deliverance* (Prov. 11:14). This does not mean we go around asking every person, "What should I do?" but it indicates the wisdom of seeking counsel from a group of believers rather than relying on one person, especially when facing significant changes or battles. Acts 15 is the record of a conference the early church held to deal with whether Gentiles could become Christians without undergoing circumcision. The conclusion was that the gospel was for Gentiles without any additional requirements. In explaining the decision of the council, the participants stated, *For it was the Holy Spirit's decision—and ours—to put no greater burden on you than these necessary things* (15:28). Once again we see the Holy Spirit guiding spiritual leaders who offered godly counsel to others.

LISTEN

As you seek to make decisions that honor God listen for what the Lord may be saying to you through life circumstances, everyday events, and other people. Listen to yourself—are you really seeking direction or simply confirmation of what you've already decided? If you've already made up your mind be willing to listen and change your mind. Welcome input, even if it's negative. If you receive criticism that isn't necessarily constructive don't pout or strike back, instead determine to learn from it, forgive the counselor for being human, and then move on.

You certainly want to respect godly direction you receive from others but spend time in solitude and prayer before acting on that counsel. Listen to the Holy Spirit as you consider whether the advice you received fits God's nature and character as revealed in His Word. Test whether the counsel you received is true, honest, pure, and would lead to loving others and glorifying God. Perfection is not a requirement for a godly counselor, but consistent progress on the journey toward a Christ-centered life is. If the counsel you receive leads you to be more self-centered, seek other counsel.

Ultimately listen to and put your trust, not in those who give you godly counsel, but in God who through His Spirit uses mature believers to advise and assist you in your journey toward Christlikeness.

What are some important decisions in your life that require godly wisdom?

Write the names of two or three spiritually mature men or women you feel you can approach to seek godly counsel.

What two questions would you like to ask those godly counselors?

CHAPTER 6

PROCLAIMING THE GOOD NEWS

HOPE FOR THE WORLD

WHY STUDY THIS LESSON? Believers are called to proclaim to the world the peace of God available only through Jesus Christ; the power to fulfill this calling is available from the Holy Spirit.

BACKGROUND PASSAGE	FOCAL PASSAGE	MEMORY VERSES
JOHN 20:19-23	JOHN 20:21-22	MATTHEW 28:18-20

A MISSION OF PEACE

In the mountainous region of south central Chad live a group of people called the Hadjeray who once lived on the plains but fled to the mountains to escape being slaughtered in war. A subgroup of the Hadjeray is the Bidio, an Islamic group of more than 60,000. Among the Bidio are about 30 Christian believers and one evangelical church. The need is great for someone to proclaim peace to these troubled people so they can flee eternal death and find refuge and salvation in Jesus for eternity.

In every town there are pockets of people who need to hear the gospel of peace. Some are English-speaking, affluent, and educated. Others do not speak English, struggle to earn a livable income, and lack any advantage that would give them hope. Both groups have something in common: they are captives of sin and need a right relationship with God.

The Bidio in Chad, the affluent, the poverty-stricken, and lost people all over the world need to know that only Jesus can save them from their sins and give them peace. But *how can they call on Him they have not believed in? And how can they believe without hearing about Him? And how can they hear without a preacher? And how can they preach unless they are sent* (Rom. 10:14-15a)?

Whose assignment is it to proclaim the gospel of peace?

As we are progressively transformed into the image of Christ, "Why am I here?" is a question answered by the realization that every believer's mission is to proclaim the peace of God through Christ to the world. The spiritual practice of being engaged in missions is not only for vocational preachers and missionaries. Those whom Jesus selected as disciples were not religious professionals. A few were fishermen, another was a tax collector, and one a zealot with strong nationalistic tendencies. What they all had in common was a commitment to Jesus, a desire to serve Him, and His call to be on mission.

According to Luke 9:1-2, what did Jesus send the twelve disciples out to do?

How were they to fulfill such a demanding assignment?

Four truths stand out in Jesus' initial commission to the Twelve: (1) The call to come to Christ is a prerequisite for being on mission for Him. (2) He equips and prepares those whom He calls out and sets aside for His mission. (3) He sends out those whom He has called. (4) The mission is kingdom-focused, life-changing, and offers victory over all that destroys. The apostles' diversity as individuals and their unity in Christ are a microcosm of the church and God's kingdom. Peoples of different backgrounds become a community on mission to bring others under the gracious rule of God.

PEACE TO YOU!

On the evening of the first Easter, 10 of the 12 apostles gathered in an unidentified location in Jerusalem. Judas Iscariot was no longer with them. Thomas wasn't there either for some unexplained reason (John 20:24). Fearful of becoming the next targets of the Jews, Jesus' followers huddled behind locked doors. Perhaps they discussed events of the past three days, regret over their unfaithful behavior, and their disappointment and confusion concerning Jesus and who they had perceived Him to be. They may have considered options for fleeing the city or returning to their former ways of life. The fearful, hopeless atmosphere in the room changed dramatically with an unexpected arrival.

Underline what Jesus said twice in John 20:19-22 below. Why might He have needed to repeat that phrase?

> 19 *In the evening of that first day of the week, the disciples were*
> *gathered together with the doors locked because of their fear of*
> *the Jews. Then Jesus came, stood among them, and said to them,*
> *"Peace to you!"* 20 *Having said this, He showed them His hands*
> *and His side. So the disciples rejoiced when they saw the Lord.* 21
> *Jesus said to them again, "Peace to you! As the Father has sent Me,*
> *I also send you."* 22 *After saying this, He breathed on them and*
> *said, "Receive the Holy Spirit."*

Jesus tried more than once to prepare His disciples for His crucifixion. Yet they seemed surprised by the turn of events and fled rather than stand by Him when He was arrested in the garden of Gethsemane. While Jesus' warning about His suffering had also included a promise of resurrection, His death weighed so heavily on their hearts that His words of life seemed not to have entered their minds. These followers of Jesus were driven by fear of what they saw rather than by faith in what was promised.

Why might Jesus' disciples have not understood His predictions about His coming death?

What made the disciples' fear so unnecessary is that just that morning Mary Magadalene had reported seeing the resurrected Jesus. Peter and John had raced to the garden tomb and seen for themselves that Jesus' body was not there (John 20:1-10). Yet Jesus' followers as a whole did not connect anything Mary, Peter, or John saw with the promise of resurrection. In fact, the reports of an empty tomb only magnified their confusion and fears.

Why didn't the disciples seem to recall Jesus' promise of resurrection?

The locked doors the disciples hid behind were evidence of the fear and uncertainty that bound them. However, locked doors and immobilizing fears are no match for Jesus. **Jesus came, stood among them** (v. 19b), and extended a greeting of peace. To assure them they were not seeing a ghost, He showed them the wounds of the crucifixion. Convinced, they **rejoiced** at seeing Him. In an instant, Jesus demonstrated His mastery over seemingly locked-up situations and His ability to bring joy in the midst of fear.

How has Jesus come to you when you have been troubled, confused, or fearful?

What difference did His presence make in your situation?

Jesus said to them again, "Peace to you" (v. 21)! This phrase was a customary Jewish greeting expressed by the word *shalom*. In this context it's more than a common greeting; it's a theological statement serving as a reminder of who Jesus was and why He ıad come. He delivered eternal peace (Isa. 9:6-7). The angels sang ›f peace at His birth (Luke 2:14). Some of His final instructions ocused on peace (John 14:27; 16:33). The apostle Paul noted that, hrough His death and resurrection, we can have peace with God Rom. 5:1; 8:6; Eph. 2:17).

Peace to us generally means the absence of conflict, but the vord means so much more. It includes the ideas of completeness, vholeness, tranquility, prosperity, and soundness in all areas of life. \ll these positive qualities result from being in a completely sound, ›eaceful, and friendly relationship with God. Being a disciple of esus Christ is much more than what you give up, don't do, or lack. Being a disciple is living a life of blessing, opportunity, purpose, and ullness (John 10:10b).

Jesus not only brought immediate calm to His stressed and fear-ul followers, but He also reinforced the eternal purpose for which He had been sent by the Father. His was a mission of peace. Sin was he reason people did not have peace with God. Jesus came to take ıway sin making peace with God possible. Peace becomes a reality n our lives when we trust in Christ. We then proclaim to others the ›eace He has given us.

What does Christ's declaration, "Peace to you!" mean to you on a daily basis?

Write down the name(s) of someone you interact with regu-arly who needs to hear about the peace the Lord gives.

The time had come for Jesus to return to the Father and for His disciples to move out into the world as His representatives to extend His mission. Being on mission is at the heart of Christian disciple-ship. Followers of Christ are to go on mission with Him, under His authority, and on His behalf.

From the outset of his Gospel, John established the theme that God sent His Son into the world. In fact, more than three dozen times in John it is said that Jesus had been sent by God the Father.

See, for example, John 1:1-18; 3:16; 4:34; 5:36; 8:42; and 17:3. In John 20:21, Jesus once more affirmed that **the Father has sent me**. His faithfulness to the Father's mission led Him to the cross. The Father's approval of His Son's mission was expressed through His bursting forth from the tomb.

Since Jesus' faithfulness to His mission sent Him to the cross, what does that imply about your faithfulness to the mission on which He sends you?

In what ways does Jesus' resurrection encourage you to be faithful to the mission even when you are pressured to forsake it?

Though Jesus' redemptive work was finished, the mission of proclamation was not yet complete; it was to be continued and effected through His followers. The mission and the message were the same but the form (or method as we might say) was different. **As**, meaning according to the same purpose, the Father had sent Jesus, He was sending them—**I also send you**. This was not a new mission. Just as Jesus came to earth to reveal the Father and provide redemption from sin, making peace with God possible, followers of Jesus Christ are sent into the world to declare God's revelation of Himself in Jesus and proclaim His message of redemption and peace.

Jesus did not hand over His mission to His followers, leaving them to themselves and their own resources. The mission was beyond their own ability both to comprehend and implement apart from an enlightenment and empowerment outside of themselves. Thus, after commissioning them, **He breathed on them** (v. 22); giving them a power that enlightened, authorized, and motivated them to carry out the task.

Jesus then exhorted His followers to **receive the Holy Spirit**. What He breathed on them was not just air discharged from the lungs; it was the Holy Spirit He had spoken about in His extended conversation with His disciples in the upper room the night of His arrest (John 14–16). As His own ministry had begun with an endowment of the Spirit (John 1:32-33), Jesus imparted to them the Spirit of God. *Receive* means to take as one's own. The grammatical form of the word suggests "start receiving."

The indwelling of the Spirit of God in the life of the believer is an ongoing experience because the Lord is constantly giving Himself and can always be counted on to be present. This breath of the Spirit in the lives of these disciples would soon become like the rush of a violent wind (Acts 2:1-2). The breathing of the Spirit introduced a mission that would become mighty in scope and effect—not limited to Jerusalem but extending to the ends of the earth. It was not just a first-century event but continues into the 21st century and will endure until Christ comes again.

How can you "start receiving" and "take as your own" the Holy Spirit each day?

How might your life be different if you lived each day in the power of the Holy Spirit?

PROCLAIM PEACE

COMMISSIONED TO PROCLAIM

Each of the gospels ends with a commission by the risen Lord to His followers and Acts begins with one (Matt. 28:18-20; Mark 16:15; Luke 24:46-47; John 20:21-22; Acts 1:8).

Compare the commissioning statements in John and Acts with Matthew 28:18-20 (below) and note what all three have in common.

> *18 Then Jesus came near and said to them, "All authority has been given to Me in heaven and on earth. 19 Go, therefore, and make disciples of all nations, baptizing them in the name of the Father*

and of the Son and of the Holy Spirit, 20 teaching them to observe everything I have commanded you. And remember, I am with you always, to the end of the age."

Matthew 28:18-20, the memory verses for this session, is perhaps the most well-known of Jesus' commissioning statements. Commonly known as the Great Commission, the core mandate is "make disciples." The other elements in the commission give instructions for how this mandate can be achieved.

- First is the "going" dimension of the commission; mobilizing believers for intentional gospel presentation.
- Next is the "baptizing" dimension; urging believers to identify with Christ and assimilating them into the life and ministry of the church.
- Last is the "teaching" dimension; teaching believers to obey the commands of the Lord; one of which is "make disciples," thus, coming full circle by leading others to be on mission themselves.

What is the "promise" dimension of the Great Commission?

How does that promise empower you to go on mission?

According to 2 Corinthians 5:14, what can compel you to go on mission to proclaim peace?

CALLED, COMPELLED, AND EMPOWERED TO PROCLAIM

The world is fallen, hopeless, bound to sin and destined to destruction. The Christian mission is to share the gospel of Christ with all peoples of the earth that they might have forgiveness of sin and enjoy a right relationship with God. The mission is an extension of Jesus' own mission, offering peace, hope, forgiveness, and eternal life. All believers are called to be on mission, compelled by love for

God, and empowered by the Holy Spirit.

Being on mission as a way of life requires that intentional daily decisions be less self-centered and more Christ-centered. That means we determine to focus on this big lost world instead of focusing on our own little worlds.

There are several keys to unlocking doors we hide behind so we can be sent out to boldly proclaim Christ's peace.

Pray—Prayer is the master key to implementing the spiritual practice of being on mission. Ask God to break your heart over the lost condition of the world. Pray for the right motivation for being involved in missions, not out of guilt or attempts to impress God and others, but because you're so compelled by love for God and others that you can't help but be involved in missions. Pray for God's power to infuse the missions endeavors of your church. Ask the Lord to raise up people to support those endeavors with their spiritual gifts, time, and finances. Pray with the willingness to be one of those people He raises up.

Pray specifically for missionaries by name, both volunteers sent out by your church and vocational missionaries sponsored by your church or denomination. You can learn specific names through printed and Internet material. Sign up for a missionary's email list to receive updates and prayer requests. Make an intentional determination to move beyond the standard "God bless the missionaries" blanket prayer.

Learn—Commit yourself to learning about God's work in the world, using resources provided by your church, a denominational missions entity, or your own research. "Adopt" a country or unreached people group in a region of the world. Learn as much as you can about them. Ask God to open doors for the gospel to enter that region. Make it personal by remembering you're not just learning about and praying for a shape on a map but for men, women, and children whom Jesus loves.

Give—Make it a habit to give generously and consistently to the mission endeavors of your church, denomination, or other mission organizations. Sponsor teenagers and others from your church to go on short- or long-term mission trips.

Go—As you pray for specific mission needs, nations, and unreached people groups, be willing to go serve and share the gospel with your unique gifts and personality. Participate in global and local missions projects. Prayerfully consider whether God is calling you to be a career missionary and answer that call joyfully. Be on mission wherever you live, work, or play. Look for opportunities to join Christ in declaring the good news, proclaiming peace, and bringing people into right relationship with Him.

Let there be no confusion as to the mission of believers of Christ on this earth: to proclaim to all peoples—at home and abroad— the good news that peace with God is available through the sacrificial death and glorious resurrection of Jesus Christ. God has given you a monumental mission, superior power through the Holy Spirit, and the glorious privilege of going to people locked behind doors of fear, sin, and hopelessness and declaring in Jesus' name, **Peace to you**!

In what ways are you joining Christ on mission to proclaim peace and redemption to a troubled world?

How can you increase your effectiveness?

CHAPTER 7

BIBLE MEDITATION

INTERNALIZING THE LIVING WORD

WHY STUDY THIS LESSON? Meditating on Scripture allows it to penetrate us and absorb its truths into us so that we follow its teachings.

BACKGROUND PASSAGE	FOCAL PASSAGE	MEMORY VERSE
JOSHUA 1:1-9	JOSHUA 1:6-9	JOSHUA 1:8

A PERSONAL WORD

Meditation! Jamie had been a Christian for several years but had never been introduced to the spiritual practice of Bible meditation. In fact, when the subject first came up she felt extremely uncomfortable as she imagined sitting cross-legged for hours, with arms folded and eyes closed. *Meditation*, she thought, *is a practice of Zen Buddhists or New Agers, not Bible-believing Christians.* Jamie read her Bible daily and participated in a weekly Bible study group. Did she really need to do more?

As Jamie listened intently to the discipleship group leader describe Bible meditation she realized the difference. The *study* of Scripture is concerned with learning about the setting of a passage, why it was written, and coming to understand what it means. The *meditation* of Scripture centers on internalizing and personalizing the passage. "The written word becomes a living word addressed to you."[1] *Wow!* Jamie thought. A *personal word for me!* Jamie committed herself to the practice of filling her mind with Scripture by pondering its meaning and absorbing its truths into her mind and heart. Yes, it took time and required discipline, but the benefits were amazing. Jamie discovered that the more she internalized Scripture her faith and commitment to Christ grew deeper, her prayers became more confident, and Christ's character flowed out of her more consistently.

Meditation on Scripture is a practice God graciously gives to spur us along on our journey toward Christlikeness. The psalmist declared, I *will meditate on Your precepts and think about Your ways* (Ps. 119:15). He expressed the intention of all those who love God's Word to meditate on it, delight in it, learn from it, encounter the Lord through it, and obey it.

What are your feelings about engaging in the spiritual practice of Bible meditation?

Pray Psalm 119:15, expressing a willingness to learn about and try the spiritual practice of meditation.

PERSONALLY PRACTICAL

The only leader Israel had known since the Exodus from Egypt was Moses. The Book of Joshua begins with the announcement that Moses had died. The Lord called out Joshua to be Moses' successor. Joshua had been a servant to Moses so he had some prior preparation for the task. Even so, he would not be allowed to ease into the role. The Lord immediately charged him to prepare the people to cross the Jordan River and take possession of the land He had long promised to them. What a task lay before him! Could he do it? Would the people accept his leadership?

According to Joshua 1:6-9 below, how would Joshua be able to accomplish such an assignment?

6 "Be strong and courageous, for you will distribute the land I
swore to their fathers to give them as an inheritance. 7 Above
all, be strong and very courageous to carefully observe the whole
instruction My servant Moses commanded you. Do not turn from
it to the right or the left, so that you will have success wherever you
go. 8 This book of instruction must not depart from your mouth;
you are to recite it day and night so that you may carefully observe
everything written in it. For then you will prosper and succeed
in whatever you do. 9 Haven't I commanded you: be strong and
courageous? Do not be afraid or discouraged, for the LORD *your*
God is with you wherever you go."

REVELATION AND EXPECTATION

In verse 5b, the Lord promised Joshua His presence, which would assure victory as he and the people moved forward to possess the land. Beginning with verse 6, God made known what He expected of Joshua. God would do His part; would Joshua do his part? Dependence on the Lord to give us victory does not justify a passive faith. In fact, faith without corresponding action is dead (Jas. 2:26). Willingness to act as God directs is evidence of the sincerity of our faith and a testimony to the depth of our convictions about God's promises.

At this point in your life is your faith more: Active? Passive?

What would be the benefit of a more active faith?

Three times the Lord challenged Joshua to **be strong and courageous** (vv. 6-7, 9). The words are very close in meaning and often used by the Lord to encourage those who are about to take on a challenging assignment. In this case, Joshua would have the privilege of being the agent of God's fulfillment of His promise concerning Israel's possession of the land. To be able to **distribute the land** God had promised **to their fathers . . . as an**

inheritance, Joshua would need strength of character, faith, and determination.

What assignment in your life is requiring you to be strong and courageous?

Where are you seeking that strength and courage?

The Lord expected Joshua **to carefully observe the whole instruction My servant Moses commanded you** (v. 7). Although Joshua's mentor Moses was no longer present, the instructions he gave lived on because they were not Moses' but the Lord's. God's instructions were far more than suggestions, guidelines, or options. They were not to be taken lightly. Joshua was to demonstrate the same strength and courage in observing those instructions as he was in leading God's people to conquer the land. He was *to carefully observe*, meaning keep watch over, be on guard concerning, be careful to practice, those instructions.

Even as we give emphasis to memorizing and meditating on God's Word, His ultimate expectation is that His Word is to be put into practice. Joshua was not to pick and choose which of the commandments he would obey but **observe the whole instruction . . . commanded you.** Finally, he was to avoid wavering or getting sidetracked along the way. **Do not turn from it to the right or the left.** In other words, stay focused.

Why does it take great strength and courage to stay focused on obeying all of God's Word?

The message is clear. The Lord had revealed His instructions and expected those who belonged to Him to heed those instructions fully and completely. Then, **you will have success wherever you go.** *Success* comes from a word that denotes wisdom and rudence. Godly success is not measured by personal achievements, ttainments, or amounts earned. It is something of much greater alue and more enduring than any of those things.

MEDITATION AND SUCCESS

he Lord continued His counsel to Joshua to prepare him for the najor leadership task of mobilizing the people to cross the Jordan River and occupy Canaan. Joshua was to rise to the occasion with trength and courage. Above all, he was to faithfully and consis-ently keep God's instructions conveyed through Moses. The Lord gave Joshua steps to take that would result in deriving the greatest enefit from His Word.

This book of instruction must not depart from our mouth (v. 8). In other words, God told Joshua, "Don't stop alking about them." We tend to talk about things that are important o us, that we enjoy, and want to know more about. Perhaps that is what is behind this statement from the Lord. Joshua was to let it be obvious to others in Israel that the instructions of the Lord were mportant to him and essential to his ability to lead. One way to einforce learning is to repeat information over and over. Joshua was o keep this Word on the "tip of his tongue," always ready to share t with those who needed to hear it and eager to teach to the next generation.

What are three subjects you enjoy talking about? Why did each item make your list?

You are to recite it day and night. It was not uncommon for he ancients to read aloud to themselves in a low or muffled tone to eflect on each word. That is in the background of the word *recite*. By extension it came to mean to ponder, imagine, or meditate. Some English Bible translations prefer the rendering "meditate" in this verse. Not only were the instructions of the Lord to be on the tip of oshua's tongue, they also were to be on "top of his mind." They were o flood his heart. His thinking and his emotions were to be under he influence of this instructive Word from the Lord. *Day and night* ndicates this was to be a constant practice for Joshua, not an occa-sional one or only when facing a major task. In order to experience the full effect of God's Word on our lives, we must be constantly seeking God's Word, internalizing it, and acting on it. That occurs when we engage in the spiritual practice of Bible meditation.

Many, like Jamie, associate meditation with non-Christian religions where people focus on emptying or purging their minds. *Biblical meditation, on the other hand, is filling the mind with truth as revealed in Holy Scripture, pondering it, and allowing it to work its way into our lives so that it affects our thinking and behavior.* Donald Whitney defines Bible meditation as "deep thinking on the truths and spiritual realities revealed in Scripture for the purposes of understanding, application, and prayer."[2] He likens meditation to preparing a cup of tea. The tea bag can be dipped into a cup of hot water repeatedly so that some tea flavor begins to affect the water. "Meditation, however, is like immersing the bag completely and letting it steep until all the rich tea flavor has been extracted and the hot water is thoroughly tinctured reddish brown."[3] As we meditate on God's Word, it "steeps" into our lives and its effects become evident to us and to those around us.

What changes might you need to make in your attitudes and activities in order to regularly meditate on God's Word?

Giving constant attention to the Lord's Word is more than religious practice; it is personally practical: **so that you may carefully observe everything written in it** (v. 8b). Once more Joshua is reminded that he is to carry out the commands and obey the instructions. Speak the Word, meditate on the Word, and do the Word.

For then you will prosper and succeed in whatever you do. Our culture usually measures prosperity in dollars and possessions and success by awards or position. Neither represents the biblical view. To *prosper* is to move toward a positive conclusion. To succeed is to live wisely and prudently. Joshua's hope of a positive conclusion in claiming the land and acting wisely as a leader would be dependent on his faithful and inflexible adherence to the instructions from the Lord.

As you think about your own Christian journey, what does it

mean for you to prosper and succeed?

PRESENCE AND CONFIDENCE

In the form of a rhetorical question, the Lord once again commanded Joshua to **be strong and courageous** and then to **not be afraid or discouraged** (v. 9). Joshua had no cause to be terrified or awed by the challenges before him. Neither did he have a reason to be dismayed or beaten down by any threats.

According to verse 9, what was to be the source of Joshua's courage and confidence?

Joshua could be strong and courageous and would prosper and succeed, not because he was highly capable and the task was easy, but by giving his undivided attention to the Lord's instructions and trusting the Lord to be with him wherever he went, no matter the circumstances. Therefore, Joshua could eagerly shoulder the leadership responsibility to which he had been called, face any tests that might come to him, and overcome any foe who challenged him.

In a time when you were afraid or discouraged what role did Scripture play in reminding you that God was present with you?

How is your confidence in moving forward on your Christian journey increased by being assured of God's constant presence?

MAKING MEDITATION PERSONAL

Joshua, like most adults, was a busy person facing a major task. Because his days were filled with crucial responsibilities, his mind needed to be filled with God's **book of instruction**—the Scripture of his day—not just by reading and learning the Law but also by taking the time to ponder it and chew on it until it became part of him. By doing so he would be prepared to move forward wisely and victoriously. In the same way, meditation on God's Word empowers us to move forward wisely and victoriously toward a Christ-centered life.

Since meditation makes the living Word a personal and personally practical word for believers, the methods of practicing meditation are personal as well. Below are listed several methods for meditating on Scripture. Several of these are adapted from the teachings of Donald Whitney.[4] These are not step-by-step legalistic procedures but rather suggestions to help you practice God's gift of meditation.

- Start by selecting a passage for meditation. The passage may be verses discovered as part of your daily Bible reading routine, something impressed upon you by the Holy Spirit, or a passage that speaks to a particular life situation or need you are facing. Don't forget familiar or favorite passages. Meditating on familiar passages often leads to seeing a fresh level of holy truth. Don't bite off more than you can chew; focus on just a few verses. In meditation, the goal is definitely quality rather than quantity.
- Invite the Holy Spirit to fill your mind and heart. Meditation is not a human endeavor or only an intellectual exercise; it is a spiritual experience.
- Read, reread, then read again the Scripture passage. Repetitive slow reading, reflecting on nuances and details of different portions of the passage, leads to an internalization of biblical truths so they have a transforming effect. Vary the way you read: silently, a whisper, or full voice. If meditating on a single verse or short passage, place the emphasis on a different word each time you read it. Think about what each emphasized word means in the context of that passage and note in your

journal what it says to you. Here is an example from John 2:5.

Do whatever He tells you.
Do **whatever** He tells you.
Do whatever **He** tells you.
Do whatever He **tells** you.
Do whatever He tells **you**.

- Use the Scripture as a prayer to the Lord either by quoting it to Him or using it to shape the direction of your prayer.
- Write a paraphrase of the passage in an effort to capture the meaning in your own words. Consider developing your own journal of paraphrases of Scripture that have come from your time of meditation.
- Determine a basic principle from the verse or passage you're meditating on—what does it teach? Consider how the text speaks to your current situation. Then look for application—what should you do in response to the principles and truths you have discovered? Some people find it helpful to follow the SOAP method—Scripture, Observation, Application, Prayer.
- Think of an illustration or object lesson that pictures or explains the text. For added benefit relay the illustration to a family member or friend.
- Create an artistic expression of the text—write a song or poem, sketch a picture.
- Ponder how the text points to Jesus.
- Mull over what questions are answered and problems are solved by the text.
- Apply Philippians 4:8 to the text looking for what is true, honorable, just, pure, lovely, commendable, excellent, and praiseworthy.
- Memorize the text. (Hopefully, this will happen automatically as you utilize various methods of meditation.)

Why put forth this kind of effort into meditating on God's Word when it's so much easier and less time-consuming to just read it? First, because God commands us to meditate on His Word and He never tells us to do anything that is not for our good and His glory. Second, it demonstrates we are serious about knowing and obeying God's Word because journeying toward Christlikeness is our life's main goal and priority.

List other reasons that will make it worth your time to meditate on God's Word.

Over a period of several days (it's not meditation if it's rushed), meditate on each of the following Scriptures, using a different method of meditation each day. Write down your thoughts, questions, and observations.

Joshua 1:6-9

Psalm 1

Psalm 119:15-18

Your favorite Scripture

[1] ~~Richard J. Foster, *Celebration of Discipline*~~: *The Path to Spiritual Growth* (New York: HarperOne, 1998), 29.

[2] Donald S. Whitney, *Spiritual Disciplines for the Christian Life* (Colorado Springs: NavPress, 1991), 48.

[3] Ibid.

[4] Adapted from the teachings of Donald. S. Whitney. See www.BiblicalSpirituality.org.

CHAPTER 8

FASTING

SATISFYING MY HUNGER FOR GOD

WHY STUDY THIS LESSON? Jesus anticipated that His followers would fast with appropriate motivation that seeks to honor God and submit to Him, rather than feeding our spiritual pride.

BACKGROUND PASSAGE	FOCAL PASSAGE	MEMORY VERSE
MATTHEW 6:1-18	MATTHEW 6:16-18	JOEL 2:12

ANCIENT NOT ARCHAIC

Sam is a believer who intentionally pursues becoming more Christ-centered through spiritual practices such as prayer, Bible study, and involvement in his community of faith. However, Sam recently encountered some challenges he just couldn't seem to gain any victory over. As he sought God's Word about these struggles, he ran across an episode in Mark 9 when Jesus explained that the disciples were unable to cast out an evil spirit because, "*This kind can come out by nothing but prayer [and fasting]*" (Mark 9:29). Sam began to wonder if he should fast about the spiritual walls he kept running into. But he hesitated because he really liked to eat and he had a lot of questions about what he'd always considered an archaic religious practice.

When his pastor stood in the pulpit Sunday morning and announced he was beginning a sermon series on fasting, Sam realized this was more than coincidence; God had something to say to him about fasting. Over the next few weeks Sam discovered the spiritual practice of fasting was, in fact, not outdated. He learned it's really not about going without food but about abstaining from legitimate activities to devote time and energy to pray intensely and focus exclusively on God. He began to grasp that not eating to satisfy physical needs can lead believers to hunger for God and crave spiritual nourishment that feeds the soul. When the pastor concluded the series with a challenge to engage in 36 hours of prayer and fasting to seek God's favor and direction on their individual lives and church body, Sam was excited to join other believer in this extremely beneficial spiritual practice.

What's the difference between fasting being an ancient spiritual practice and an archaic religious practice?

Which of those labels have you most often attached to the concept of fasting and why?

WHEN YOU FAST

As a result of His teaching, preaching, and healing, Jesus' popularity grew rapidly. Jesus wanted those who were attracted to Him to understand what He intended for those who follow Him and expressed His expectations in what is known as the Sermon on the Mount in Matthew 5-7. He declared His followers were to demonstrate a righteousness that exceeded that of the scribes and Pharisees (Matt. 5:20). Given that these two groups were considered the paragons of righteous living and religious practice, to exceed them seemed impossible. Jesus gave six examples to illustrate what He meant. Primarily the examples focused on how people were to relate to one another. However, He also gave attention to some religious practices considered marks of piety and challenged His disciples to examine the motives behind each practice.

Read Mathew 6:16-18 below. Then underline the beginning phrases in the first two verses. What do you find significant about these phrases?

> *16 "Whenever you fast, don't be sad-faced like the hypocrites. For*
> *they make their faces unattractive so their fasting is obvious to*
> *people. I assure you: They've got their reward! 17 But when you*
> *fast, put oil on your head, and wash your face, 18 so that you don't*
> *show your fasting to people but to your Father who is in secret.*
> *And your Father who sees in secret will reward you.*

THE ASSUMPTION

Similar to the way He introduced instructions on prayer (vv. 5, 7), Jesus began His instructions for this practice with **whenever you fast**. Jesus assumed His followers would fast just as He assumed they would pray. Since the goal of our spiritual journey is to be like Jesus and since Jesus Himself fasted (Matt. 4:2; Luke 4:2), it's safe to assume fasting is still a commended, though not commanded, practice for believers to engage in today.

Jesus didn't give instructions on the actual method of fasting because it was a common practice in His day. Refraining from eating for a period of time as an act of devotion, confession, and drawing nearer to God was part of the Hebrews' religious heritage. The Day of Atonement was an annual fast day all Jews were expected to observe. Other special fast days might be held by the whole community as expressions of national mourning and repentance. Generally, however, fasting was a personal act of spiritual concentration. Strict Jews, such as the Pharisees, fasted two days a week (Luke 18:12). Jesus' original hearers already knew how to fast physically but they needed instructions on how to fast properly with the right motive.

THE MOTIVE

As an individual practice, fasting was intended to be a voluntary, personal act of devotion before God. However the **hypocrites**, a word that originally referred to performers, "play-acted" religion and made their fasting a **sad-faced** public display. They wanted others to know what they were doing. They didn't just wear their religion on their sleeves; they literally wore it on their faces. They took on gloomy, somber looks, distorted their appearance by not washing or refreshing their skin with oil, and created the impression of being pale and weak from hunger by using ashes to discolor their complexion.

So their fasting is obvious to people. A kind of wordplay exists in this sentence. The hypocrites hid or distorted their real faces so their fake faces would be seen. What they did was for appearance' sake to receive the recognition of people who would be awed at such devotion. If what they sought was the recognition of other people, Jesus assured them, **they've got their reward!** That would be the only benefit that would come to them. God would not be impressed.

But when you fast sets the stage for an emphatic contrast. Jesus expected the opposite from His disciples. They were not to put on piety like an actor putting on a mask. Rather than look sad, look happy. They were to refresh themselves by anointing their heads with **oil**, a sign of celebration and happiness. In addition, **wash your face**, which obviously would give the individual a clean, fresh, and more appealing look. While the hypocrites altered their appearance to receive accolades from those who saw them, Jesus exhorted His followers to take extra measures to brighten their countenance **so that you don't show your fasting to people**. Here is a principle of fasting: it is a personal, private matter; something not shared with others.

Even though some spiritual practices are personal and private, does this mean you are to keep your entire spiritual life private? Why or why not?

In Sam's case, it was beneficial for his small group to discuss their experiences with the corporate 36-hour fast. One man shared how he became very aware of his proud self-sufficiency when he discovered how difficult it was, not to abstain from eating lunch, but from working through his lunch hour and spending that time praying instead. The other participants suggested that the next time he fasted he could go on a prayer walk during lunch to get away from the phone and computer. The group was really impacted when a woman whose job was being phased out said she'd chosen to fast from pessimism and focus on trusting God to open doors. None of the believers shared about their fast in an attempt to impress but to encourage each other. They didn't moan about what they had missed but celebrated what God had done in their lives as they engaged in this spiritual discipline.

THE BLESSING

Although it was not inappropriate for the believers in Sam's small group to share about their experiences in a corporate fast, Jesus clearly taught most fasts are to be kept private between the believer and the **Father who is in secret** (v. 18). Some Bible translations prefer the rendering "unseen." Just because God is unseen does not mean He does not see us. He **sees in secret**, meaning He sees more than what we are physically. He looks into the unseen, the deepest recesses of our being. He sees into our hearts and knows what is most important to us. He looks into our minds and knows our motives. He identifies our spirits and knows without a doubt if they are compatible with His Spirit.

The truth that God knows my heart and mind¬¬—

Challenges me because

Comforts me because

God is far more concerned with the attitude of the one fasting rather than the act itself. Others may not know if a person is fasting, but the Father does because He knows all things. In response, He will **reward** them. Whether His reward is immediate or in the future is not specified nor should it matter. Neither should we read the promise of reward to suggest we earn God's blessings by doing religious things. Whenever and however God rewards His children for their faithfulness, we should always see them as a blessing of grace.

Genuine fasting is not an attempt to impress God, manipulate Him into doing what we want, or sway Him to our way of thinking. Rather it is a means of emptying ourselves so we become more attuned to hear God and begin to think with Christ's mind-set. God promises to reward, bless, and honor our efforts to draw closer to Him. Fasting provides great insight into what our lives revolve around, so a great reward of this practice is becoming less self-centered and more Christ-centered. Other blessings include: a more powerful, effective, and focused prayer life; deliverance from habits, fears, and other chains that have you bound up; and guidance for important decisions.

Fasting brings impurities in your life to the surface. In response to his pastor's challenge to record what God said to them during the 36-hour fast Sam journaled, "*I've become aware I feel pretty entitled to comfort—that it's my right to feel free of all discomfort, including hunger. Ouch! Learning to rely on the Holy Spirit to go a few more hours without food is teaching me to rely on His power to go beyond myself when things get uncomfortable rather than just giving up. I hear the Lord saying, 'You need to hang on and not give up when things get tough. I work best through weak people.*'" This word from God was a real blessing in Sam's life, giving him faith and courage to persevere through the challenges he was facing.

What blessings from fasting would you most like to experience in your life?

INCREASE UNDERSTANDING

Although fasting to lose weight or detox the body has gained attention in recent years, fasting for spiritual purposes has often been neglected or completely dismissed. That neglect often stems from fear which almost always stems from ignorance. If you're uncertain about fasting, that's nothing to feel guilty or pressured about, but you can increase your understanding of this very beneficial spiritual practice.

Expand your understanding of fasting in Scripture by reviewing Old and New Testament references to the practice, such as:

Leviticus 16:29-31; Nehemiah 1:4-7; 9:1-2; Psalm 35:13; Isaiah 58:6-10; Joel 2:12; Matthew 4:1-11; 9:14-17; 1 Corinthians 7:5; and Acts 13:1-3. Read and meditate on the verses. Determine reasons for and benefits of fasting from those passages. Write your own paraphrase or develop a summary statement of truths about fasting from the verse(s).

Christian leaders through the ages have practiced fasting, including Jonathan Edwards, John Wesley, and Martin Luther. Look up and read what they had to say about fasting. Read the chapters on fasting in *Celebration of Discipline* by Richard J. Foster and *Spiritual Disciplines for the Christian Life* by Donald S. Whitney to gain explanations of and suggestions for fasting.

MOTIVATION, MEANS, AND METHOD

Our lives are crowded with good things and good activities. Sometimes we need to give exclusive attention to the most important thing—nurturing our relationship with God. There is perhaps no better way to do that than fasting. In a fast we relinquish those things that may control us as a way of declaring we want our lives to be under God's control. To incorporate the spiritual practice of fasting in our lives, we can consider the motivation, means, and method, and then make an intentional commitment to fast on our journey toward Christlikeness.

MOTIVATION

Decide the motivation for your fast—remembering that the main goal is to center yourself around Christ and His will. Determine if God's purpose for you to fast is: for repentance and confession of sin; to focus more attention on prayer and meditation; to seek God's guidance for a decision; to deal with grief or a heartbreaking situation; to seek God's protection over something that threatens you; as an act of humility before the Lord; to seek divine intervention and strength to overcome a temptation that has come upon you; or as an intense, private time simply to worship God.

List what you feel God is leading you to specifically pray for during the fast. Certainly you can fast for personal reasons but since the goal of fasting is to be less self-centered, include prayers for others, including your church.

MEANS

Determine the means of your fast by deciding what you will abstain from. It may be food or something else that is prominent in your life that, while an acceptable behavior, prevents you from spending time focusing on the things of the Lord. Even people who cannot fast from food for medical reasons can still fast. (If you have health issues and want to try fasting from food, check with your doctor first.) You can choose under the Spirit's direction another means of fasting—TV, social media, a hobby, an addictive app on your mobile device, even sleep—in order to focus on God. For example: Do you watch a baseball game every night during the summer? Consider a week of not watching games or determine not to watch a game on Tuesday evenings throughout the summer months.

Equally as important as determining the nature of your fast is deciding how you will spend the time made available by abstaining from that activity. That may include Scripture reading, meditation, prayer, listening, journaling, music, or whatever else helps you focus on God to be spiritually cleansed and nourished in your spirit.

Underline in the verses below appropriate actions that accompany fasting.

> *Even now—this is the Lord's declaration—turn to Me with all your heart, with fasting, weeping, and mourning* (Joel 2:12).

> *She did not leave the temple complex, serving God night and day with fasting and prayers* (Luke 2:37).

> 2 *As they were ministering to the Lord and fasting, the Holy Spirit said, "Set apart for Me Barnabas and Saul for the work I have called them to."* 3 *Then after they had fasted, prayed, and laid hands on them, they sent them off* (Acts 13:2-3).

METHODS

There are two basic methods of fasting from food. A partial fast is a restriction of diet but not total abstinence from food and water. If you are new to fasting it would be wise to start with a partial fast. Perhaps abstain from eating lunch every day for a week. Try to work up to going 36 hours without food. Start by fasting from dinner one evening, fast the entire next day, drinking only water (and fruit juice if necessary), and break the fast the next morning.

A complete fast is abstaining from food and water for extreme circumstances such as in Esther 4:16 and Acts 9:9. Richard Foster emphasizes a complete fast should not be engaged in without a clear command from God and never longer than three days.[1] The length of time is not the issue. What's important is what you do with the time and your attitude concerning the practice. Don't focus on what's happening to your body—the hunger or the fascination of trying this new practice—instead focus on what's going on in your heart between you and God.

As much as possible, determine to keep your fast between you and the Lord. Calling attention to your fast by pointing it out to others is the kind of thing Jesus warned against in Matthew 6:16-18. Sometimes trying to keep a fast private draws more attention than simply acknowledging you are fasting and not making a big deal out of it. If your family normally eats the evening meal together, casually mention you are fasting and then spend that time either in prayer or sitting with your family as you sip some water. The point isn't so much to keep it a secret as to not draw attention to yourself.

In those times when you're really missing whatever you've given up focus on the outcome of the spiritual practice of fasting: It is putting you into a posture where you can hear God clearly and allow Him to transform you more into the image of His Son. Fasting empties you of yourself so there's more room for Jesus. Foster says, "Fasting can bring breakthroughs in the spiritual realm that will never happen in any other way. It is a means of God's grace and blessing that should not be neglected any longer."[2]

When you sense God is leading you to fast, make this commitment:

Under the Spirit's leadership I commit to fast:

For this Motivation

By this Means

With this Method

Signed: ______________________

---

[1] Richard J. Foster, *Celebration of Discipline: The Path to Spiritual Growth* (New York: HarperOne, 1998), 50.
[2] Ibid, 60.

CHAPTER 9

JOY AND CELEBRATION

EVIDENCE OF A CHANGED HEART

WHY STUDY THIS LESSON? The Bible teaches that we can have joy even in the midst of life's trials (Jas 1:2) and joy is evidence of the Holy Spirit at work in our lives (Gal. 5:22).

BACKGROUND PASSAGE	FOCAL PASSAGE	MEMORY VERSE
PHILIPPIANS 4	PHILIPPIANS 4:4-9	PHILIPPIANS 4:4

CELEBRATE!

The sunburned pastor shared the excitement he'd experienced at a college football game the day before. Every time the home team scored the cheerleaders would ask, "Whose house?" In one big roar the fans would respond, "Our house!" The pastor challenged the congregation, "Sports fans shouldn't be the only people who get to celebrate. When I ask, 'Whose house?' I want you to stand and yell, 'His house!'" It took a couple of tries to get people to loosen up but the end result, besides some nervous giggles, was a transformed atmosphere and a greater understanding that believers can rejoice and celebrate because Christ lives in His people.

Joy and celebration are key practices in our journey toward Christlikeness. The practice of joy is often personal while celebration is usually a communal practice as we join with fellow believers to celebrate the Lord and all He has done for us. Rejoicing and celebrating are crucial in empowering us to overcome the discouragements that inevitably come against us as we travel through this life. The prospect of joy can drive us forward even when the going is tough because we know God is increasingly conforming us into the image of His Son *who for the joy that lay before Him endured a cross and despised the shame and has sat down at the right hand of God's throne* (Heb. 12:2b).

REJOICE!

Paul wrote the letter known as the Book of Philippians when he was in prison facing the possibility of execution. Although that seems to be a legitimate excuse for not being joyful, the entire letter is permeated with joy. Paul had obviously discovered the secret to experiencing true joy despite less-than-ideal circumstances.

According to Philippians 4:4-9 (below), what are some key elements to rejoicing?

> *4 Rejoice in the Lord always. I will say it again: Rejoice! 5 Let*
> *your graciousness be known to everyone. The Lord is near. 6 Don't*
> *worry about anything, but in everything, through prayer and petition with thanksgiving, let your requests be made known to*
> *God. 7 And the peace of God, which surpasses every thought, will*
> *guard your hearts and minds in Christ Jesus. 8 Finally brothers,*
> *whatever is true, whatever is honorable, whatever is just, whatever is pure, whatever is lovely, whatever is commendable —if there is any moral excellence and if there is any praise—dwell on*
> *these things. 9 Do what you have learned and received and heard*
> *and seen in me, and the God of peace will be with you.*

ALWAYS

Earlier in the letter Paul had alluded to the pressure the church was experiencing from external opponents (1:27-30; 2:15; 3:2). Then in 4:2-3, he addressed an internal issue that threatened the unity of the ellowship. The situation had the potential to discourage the believ-rs and rob them of their joy of serving Christ.

Generally, how do situations around you affect your disposition?

Against the backdrop of external pressure and internal tension the postle urged believers to **rejoice in the Lord always** (v. 4). Notice that *rejoice* is an action; a discipline to be practiced by those who are *in the Lord*. The preposition *in* suggests position and relationship. *Always* means in all situations, even difficult ones. This does not mean we deny the reality of our problems, but rise above hem because we know we are in right relationship with the Lord nd are convinced He is sovereign over all things. Christian joy is sense of self-worth, well-being, and fulfillment that can only be known by being in Christ. Paul felt strongly that believers are to live with an attitude of overcoming joy. So he repeated, **I will say it again: Rejoice!**

What does it mean to you to be in the Lord?

How does that give you reason to rejoice despite the situation?

SURRENDER

The initial decision to follow Christ is the beginning of a journey oward growing to be more like Him. The journey is not a series of prescribed steps of becoming loving, then joyful, then patient, and so forth, until we arrive at the pinnacle of our spiritual lives. Christian discipleship is a dynamic experience, a spiritual adventure of walking day-to-day in the Lord. The relationship of the attributes of a Christian disciple is seen in the imagery of "the fruit of the Spirit" n Galatians 5:22-23. The use of the singular noun "fruit' suggests hese are not individual attributes for which we are to strive but the sum of virtues that define what it means to belong to Christ Jesus.

Cut open an apple and list its attributes—color, shape, firmness, texture, degree of juiciness. Take a bite and describe the taste; is it sweet or sour? Review all the listed attributes. Which made the fruit an apple?

You most likely observed that it took all the attributes to make the fruit an apple. In a similar way it is the presence of each attribute of "the fruit of the Spirit" that identifies a person as a follower of Chris This does not mean a believer possesses each item in its fullness. Discipleship is the process of growing in each of those attributes as we submit more and more to the Holy Spirit. These attributes of discipleship interact with each other in such a way to create the whole of what it is to be a disciple.

Joy is one of the attributes developed through the Holy Spirit that sets the believer apart from an unredeemed world. It is a gift of the Holy Spirit, not something you create within yourself. However when you choose the way of Christ, joy is the inevitable result. Paul exhorted believers to keep on living in and celebrating the blessed state of joy they know in the Lord. When your heart is filled with jo you can approach life differently.

According to Philippians 4:5-7, when your life is filled with joy, how will you approach:

People?

Troubling situations?

Believers can relate to others with graciousness because the joy we have in our hearts overcomes attitudes of selfishness, jealousy, or envy. We can rejoice and treat others with kindness because we know **the Lord is near** (v. 5) in the sense that He is present in ou lives and in the sense that His return is near.

Iow does the reality of Christ's nearness give you reason to ejoice?

elievers who fully surrender their lives to Christ choose not to **vorry about anything**. Worry kills joy but is overcome by faith ı Christ. We can rejoice in the Lord when we are convinced He nows, cares, and acts in ways that are in our best interest. Therefore, ve do not constantly worry about life issues.

Read Matthew 6:25-34. How did Jesus teach His followers to nanage their anxieties?

Iow does Paul's message echo Jesus' teachings?

o what are we to do with our cares and anxieties? Do we ignore hem, smile big, and pretend they don't exist? Do we just harden urselves and become emotionally insensitive or spiritually callous? Do we adopt a whatever-will-be-will-be attitude? Not at all. We eal with **everything**—all of life's issues and cares—**through rayer and petition** and **let** our **requests be made known o God.** Whenever we feel anxiety coming on we surrender control f that situation to God. We share our concerns with Him, ask for rovision, protection, and guidance, listen to His assurances and irections, and wait on Him to answer in His perfect timing. The ntire experience of coming before the Lord in prayer is **with** an ttitude of **thanksgiving**.

Vhat can you thank God for when life seems filled with only urdens and heartache?

Iow can that gratitude lead you to *Rejoice in the Lord always*?

The joy of being in the Lord leads a believer to know the **peace of God** (v. 7). *Peace*, meaning fullness and harmony in life, is of **God**. It belongs to Him and has its sole source in Him. God's peace is so superior that it **surpasses every thought**. It cannot be completely comprehended by human reason or fully described in human language.

When have you been overwhelmed by the peace of God in the midst of a trial?

How would you describe to others the peace you felt?

Even if God's peace is beyond explanation, its effectiveness is unquestioned. God's peace **will guard your hearts and minds**. Paul may have been chained to a Roman guard when he wrote the Philippian letter and that may be why he used the military term *guard* to describe God's peace. Just as a garrison of soldiers stood watch over a city to protect it from attack, so God's peace will stand guard and prevent worry and fear from invading the *hearts and minds* of believers who surrender all things to Him in prayer. What a reason to rejoice!

THINK

Christ's followers have a responsibility in knowing God's joy and peace. There are actions we can and must take in order to *rejoice in the Lord always*. One such action is to **dwell on these things** (v. 8c), meaning we are to take an inventory of, to take into account, or to think on six qualities that create an environment conducive to knowing the joy and peace that come from following Jesus.

Consider the things we often dwell on—what that person said to us, what we'd like to say back to them, the what-ifs of uncertain situations, self-pity, worry about cars, bills, kids, and on and on. Dwelling on such matters steals our joy. If we want to live in an environment of joy we've got to turn our thinking around and dwell on what's positive. No matter the situation we can remind ourselves of what we know to be **true** about Christ and His love and care or us. We don't dwell on how we can get our way but how we can ehave in ways that are **honorable** and **just**, conforming to ;od's standard of right behavior. We think on what is **pure** in that ituation—how we can remain without fault so no one will have ny grounds for accusations. We strive under the power of the Holy pirit to think about and be what is **lovely**—pleasing, acceptable, nd winsome—and **commendable**—gracious, well-spoken of, vith a good reputation.

Since **there is moral excellence and praise** in these six irtues, we are to make it a habit to think about them. Don't forget hem or ignore them. This kind of right thinking will lead to right ractice which will lead to joy.

ince thinking influences practice, what does this imply bout the discipleship strategy required to grow to be more :hrist-like?

)BEY

'aul didn't expect believers to be passive but active in pursuing joy; here are things we can **do** (v. 9), a word that means to exercise, ractice, or be busy with. Paul urged the Philippian believers to be usy with **what you have learned and received and heard nd seen in me.** Paul was confident and comfortable in offering imself as a model for how to live joyfully, not because he was the ource of joy, but because he had experienced joy through obedince to Christ. A joyful journey is marked by obedience.

ccording to John 15:10-11, what does Jesus desire for you?

Iow is that connected to obedience?

Right practice that comes from right thinking results in the **God of peace** (v. 9b) being with us. "God dwells with those who think holy houghts and do right deeds, and he brings peace."[1] His presence nd peace lead us to rejoice which then leads us to celebrate.

What are ways you celebrate the Lord and His blessing in your life?

How does your church celebrate God's blessings together?

HAVE A PARTY!

Not every believer is comfortable with the idea of corporate celebration. Certainly there is a need for decorum and reverence in worship, but that doesn't have to mean dry and boring. The Old Testament is full of instances of God's people celebrating together with great joy. One such instance is found in the Book of Nehemiah. Nehemiah had led the people to rebuild the wall around Jerusalem. Upon completion of the project, Nehemiah and Ezra assembled the people together for a reading of God's Word. Upon hearing the Word, the people were convicted of their sins and repented in tears.

Read Nehemiah 8:8-12. What did Nehemiah urge the people to do instead of mourn?

God gave His people permission to have a party! The teaching of His Word was intended to make them glad rather than sad. They were to demonstrate the joy of their renewed relationship with Him by feasting and sending gifts of food to others. God wants you to laugh, have fun, enjoy good food, and rejoice in Him with others. Then when you leave a time of corporate celebration, allow that joy in the Lord to remain in your life, sustaining and strengthening you to continue serving the Lord and obeying His Word no matter what life might throw at you.

How has your joy in Christ sustained you during a difficult time? How has that increased your joy in the Lord?

God wants you to have joy, and not just a little bit of joy, but joy to the fullest. Joy is a state of the heart and mind that results from being in right relationship with God through Jesus Christ. That's different from happiness which is a feeling in response to favorable circumstances. When circumstances change to something less favorable, the feeling of happiness may decrease or dissipate altogether. But Jesus never changes, so a believer can rejoice in the Lord even in the midst of difficulty. Celebration is acknowledging the joy and the relationship through festive activity—whether that is a party, a feast, an hour devoted to singing praise songs, or maybe even cheering for Jesus in a worship service.

There is not a single area of life that does not benefit from the practice of joy and celebration. Laughter is one of the best prescriptions for healing body, mind, and soul. Celebration puts our lives and problems into perspective, gives us an appreciation for life, and reminds us that *This is the day the* L*ORD* *has made; let us rejoice and be glad in it* (Ps. 118:24). It also assures us that even in this sinful world there is still much good to celebrate because God is in control. Rejoicing and celebrating benefits our social lives as well—a joyful person is far more pleasant to be around than a sad sack.

How does reviewing and reveling in God's goodness benefit you?

IT'S MY DECISION

God desires that you have joy but the decision to be joyful is up to you. Joy and celebration are spiritual practices that you can intentionally choose to include in your everyday life. So to cultivate joy, make deliberate choices to trust God rather than be anxious, to pray rather than fret, and to dwell on godly and positive rather than negative thoughts. Determine to be grateful rather than grumble. When life is getting you down follow the advice of the old hymn and count your blessings.

Learn to let loose and celebrate the blessings of being in Christ. When it's time to sing in celebration with your church family—SING! It doesn't matter if you can't carry a tune. It doesn't even matter if you don't like the song. You're celebrating God, not the music. If you feel like you've forgotten how to celebrate—watch little children. Nobody has to tell them how to celebrate. They laugh, dance, skip, sing, and hug without reservation.

Celebrate Christian festivals and holy days with other believers. The world may have commercialized many of those festivals but that doesn't mean we have to give them up. Take back those glorious events for the Lord and make them what God intended them to be by joyfully celebrating His goodness and mighty acts. It's OK to have feasts and give gifts—remember God gives us permission to have parties to celebrate Him.

Make family events like birthdays, weddings, and anniversaries opportunities to demonstrate joy in the Lord. Be creative. Come up with things that are meaningful to you, your family and friends, or your church that allow you to laugh, rejoice, and celebrate life, relationships, and God's goodness.

We can celebrate even when life isn't perfect because our joy isn't grounded in what we have or what happens to us—those can change in an instant. We celebrate because our joy is grounded in the Lord who has promised I *will never leave you or forsake you and who is the same yesterday, today, and forever* (Heb. 13:5,8).

Lord, I rejoice in you because...

I will celebrate the Lord's goodness with my family and church family this week by...

---

[1] Ray Frank Robbins. *Philippians: Rejoice in the Lord* (Nashville: Convention Press, 1980), 132.

CHAPTER 10

SIMPLICITY AND CONTENTMENT

WHAT DO I MOST VALUE?

WHY STUDY THIS LESSON? Followers of Jesus are called to value the eternal over the temporal and material, and to practice contentment with the Lord's provisions.

BACKGROUND PASSAGE	FOCAL PASSAGE	MEMORY VERSES
MATTHEW 6	MATTHEW 6:19-34	MATTHEW 6:19-21

LESS IS MORE

Patricia and Jack agreed they needed to simplify their lives. They sorted through all the stuff that had accumulated in various storage areas of their house. Things once considered treasures or necessities made their way to trash bins or charity collection boxes. They were surprised to discover the house they thought was too small had plenty of space. Next they developed a plan for evaluating their purchases to determine if they met real needs or satisfied wants. In time, they learned they could be content with less and found great joy in being able to redirect their resources, time, and efforts toward more worthy endeavors. Their simpler lifestyle led them to understand and agree that *godliness with contentment is a great gain* (1 Tim. 6:6).

On a scale of 1 to 10 (with 1 being not at all and 10 being completely) where do you rank yourself on the contentment scale?

Why would godly contentment be a great gain in your life?

Patricia and Jack's experience illustrates something many of us may need to do in our lives. Jesus spoke to the need of eliminating that which clutters our lives and prevents us from focusing on the most important thing in life: our relationship with God. Jesus challenged His followers to make some deliberate choices to practice a simplicity that leads to biblical contentment.

EITHER—OR

Take the time to read Matthew 6:19-34 in your Bible. List either-or choices every person must make. Spend time praying and journaling about which choices you have most often made and which choices you'd like to make.

Matthew 6:19-21 Either ____________ or ____________.

Matthew 6:22-24 Either ____________ or ____________.

Matthew 6:25-34 Either ____________ or ____________.

TWO TREASURES: WHICH WILL I COLLECT? (MATT. 6:19-21)

Wealth in the ancient world was measured in terms of property, livestock, grain, precious metals, and luxurious clothing, all of which were temporal and subject to being destroyed by **moth and rust** or stolen by **thieves**. Jesus warned against hoarding possessions for personal use and measuring human worth according to the volume of goods owned. One natural disaster, stock market collapse, or company downsizing can wipe out all of a person's **treasures** on earth in an instant. Depending on possessions and wealth is a vulnerable, insecure way to live.

In contrast, Jesus urged His followers to collect for themselves **treasures in heaven** that can't be destroyed or stolen. Spiritual treasures are anything we can take with us beyond the grave, "holiness of character, obedience to all of God's commandments, souls won for Christ, and disciples nurtured in the faith."[1]

Jesus expressed His true point of concern, **For where your treasure is, there your heart will be also**. He knew your affections, interests, time, and other resources would be directed to and invested in what you treasure most. Jesus treasures you and wants you to fully experience His life, joy, and peace. The apostle Paul would later write, *Set your minds on what is above, not on what is on the earth* (Col. 3:2). The choice is between two treasures: earthly treasures or heavenly treasures. Which will you choose?

Would life be simpler or more complicated if you focused more on collecting treasures in heaven? Why?

TWO MASTERS: WHOM WILL I SERVE? (MATT. 6:22-24)

Jesus' analogy of **good** and **bad** eyes represents two perspectives or views of life. In Jewish literature, a good eye represented generosity; the bad eye represented jealousy or greed. To see with a "good eye" is to see life clearly and act generously; to see with a "bad eye" is to have a dark view of life and be driven by greed. The condition of the eye indicates which master a person is devoted to: **God** or **money**.

In the slave culture of the New Testament period, it was common understanding that **no one can be a slave of two masters**. A slave was the exclusive property of his master and expected to give him exclusive service. A slave would either **hate one and love the other, or be devoted to one and despise the other.** There was no such place for divided loyalties. Jesus' use of hyperbole (*hate* versus *love*) was to emphasize the seriousness of the choice to be made. In no way and under no terms could a person serve two masters.

Those who desire to follow Christ must decide which master they will serve. Many believers declare they serve God, but an examination of their checkbooks, calendars, and daily practices frequently proves otherwise. If we choose God, our money, time, and activities are given over to Him and used for His good purposes. The choice is between two masters: God or stuff. Which will you choose?

How can people with little money still be controlled by and devoted to money?

How might serving God rather than money be a simpler way to live?

TWO LIFESTYLES: WHICH WILL YOU CHOOSE? (MATT. 6:25-34)

Focusing on wealth says, "I don't need God." Worry says, "I can't trust God." Neither is a simple way to live. **This is why I tell you** suggests Jesus was about to reveal yet one more decision to be made: Will we choose a lifestyle that seeks and trusts God or seeks and worries about things?

Most people—then and now—would agree **what you will eat or what you will drink and what you will wear** are basic matters. However, as important as they may be, Jesus challenged the view that they were the most important things.

What was Jesus emphasizing with His question, Isn't life more than food and the body more than clothing?

Jesus was teaching outdoors, so to illustrate His point He drew attention to **birds** and **wildflowers**. Birds industriously seek food for themselves and their young but are still dependent on natural sources for food and shelter. **Wildflowers** are even less able to provide for themselves than birds. All they need is under control of the Heavenly Father who has not forgotten them.

Yes is the implied answer to, **Aren't you worth more than they?** Human beings are created in God's image and have a special role in His eternal purpose. If God provides for the smallest and most transitory of His creation, like birds and grass, then He surely can be counted on to care for people who are at the zenith of His created order.

How has God provided for your needs just in the past month?

Jesus offered two options for living life. One option is driven by **worry**. A lifestyle of worry is unproductive and denies God's goodness and faithfulness to His children. Those who worry show themselves to have **little faith**.

Idolaters devote all their energy to finding ways to satisfy their material needs. This obsessive search inevitably leads to worry, for people will never be satisfied with what they find. Followers of Jesus on the other hand can be confident the **heavenly Father knows** and will provide our basic needs. Not only are we relieved of the pressure brought on by worry, but we are also able to devote our energy to more God-honoring efforts.

Do you agree or disagree with the description of worry as "practical atheism"? Why?

The second option for living life is to live by faith. Jesus described this way as choosing to **seek first the kingdom of God and His righteousness.** The phrase *kingdom of God* refers to His sovereign rule. *His righteousness* refers to the right way of living according to God's superior standard. Notice the contrast. Those who worry are like *idolaters* who **eagerly seek . . . things**. The faithful *seek* to be under God's reign and live according to His standards. The former focuses on temporal stuff. The latter is concerned with an eternal relationship. The former worries about being without things. The latter are confident all these things will be provided.

Jesus was not implying His followers are to be insensitive toward human needs nor was He calling us to passive living. Not all our money problems will be solved by waiting on God while we sit by idly. Neither does this passage mean God will give us everything we want or that we will prosper. A chosen lifestyle of simplicity is not about what you have or don't have; it's about who you trust. You can live without a lot of money and things and still not be practicing simplicity if you're fretting, because that's still focusing on things instead of God. Jesus declared those who seek Him can live with full trust in God and not be controlled by an obsession for the things of the world. Trusting and seeking God leads to confidence.

How might a biblically confident life be a simpler life?

The closing admonition is **don't worry about tomorrow**. Jesus was not prohibiting planning for the future; however, He did say don't worry about it. The concerns of the future belong to tomorrow; they are not yours. **Each day has enough trouble of its own** without you reaching ahead to worry about things that may or may not even happen. Little is gained by carrying forward yesterday's worries either. Focus on the present. Even then, don't worry; trust God.

The spiritual practice of simplicity and contentment begins with the inner simplicity of mind and heart that chooses to keep first things first. Jesus promises when we choose to single-heartedly seek God's rule in our lives, all the other things we need will be provided. The choice is between two lifestyles: You can live with trust, seeking God's agenda. Or you can live with worry, seeking things and your agenda. Which will you choose?

What do you most worry about and why?

How would trusting God change things for you?

How will you commit that worry to God?

COMPLICATED TO CONTENTED

The apostle Paul declared, *If anyone else thinks he has grounds for confidence in the flesh, I have more: circumcised the eighth day; of the nation of Israel, of the tribe of Benjamin, a Hebrew born of Hebrews; regarding the law, a Pharisee; regarding zeal, persecuting the church; regarding the righteousness that is in the law, blameless* (Phil. 3:4-5). Paul could attest to the fact that being everything and having everything gets really complicated.

It wasn't until he was transformed by Jesus and chose to simplify his life by first seeking God's kingdom that Paul became a contented man. Even then contentment did not come naturally; he had to learn to *be content in whatever circumstances I am.... whether in abundance or in need* (Phil. 4:11-12).

Read Philippians 4:10-13. How can the secret Paul learned lead to contentment?

How does a person learn that secret?

Paul could live contentedly through the ups and downs of life because he didn't base his confidence in money or things. There was no point complicating his life with worry because he was confident God would meet his needs. He wanted the Philippian believers to have the same assurance so he wrote, "*And my God will supply all your needs according to His riches in glory in Christ Jesus*" (4:19).

How would your life be simplified if you fully believed the promise of Philippians 4:19?

CONTENTED AND LIBERATED

Simplicity is an inward reality that results in an outward lifestyle. It involves seeking first God's kingdom and then placing all other things in their proper perspective. Simplicity challenges us to live free of the spirit of acquisition. Choosing a lifestyle of simplicity leads us to practice contentment. Recognizing true satisfaction does not come from the things of this world but from an unwavering trust in the Lord, fully convinced He will take care of us and provide for all our needs.

Life centered in money and things becomes more chaotic with each passing day because we've got to continually protect, maintain, and replace that stuff. We no longer own things, they own us. The spiritual practice of simplicity sets us free from that bondage because it clears away all the stuff. Then we can get into a position to hear God clearly and allow Him to transform us so that our lives center in Christ. A Christ-centered life is contented rather than chaotic because it's controlled by the only One who can see all of life clearly and provide for us perfectly. A life of simplicity and contentment is a liberated joyful life.

How could a lifestyle of simplicity and contentment liberate you from the tyranny of:

Yourself?

Others?

Things?

LIVING SIMPLY AND CONTENTED

We can quit making life so complicated and cluttered and instead calmly strive for simplicity. Doing so requires adopting a biblical mind-set that rejects rampant materialism and refuses to find identity or worth in stuff. It will involve learning to live contentedly without what we thought were needs but are actually just wants or luxuries. We really can intentionally cut back on lifestyle habits that are ingrained in us by our culture and experience greater simplicity and true godly contentment.

The practice of simplicity needs to come with a couple of warn-ng labels. God wants His people to enjoy the bounty and beauty of His creation, not be miserably poor. The spiritual practice of simplic-y is not legalistic asceticism. When a person seeks simplicity over God's kingdom, it becomes as much of an idol as materialism. Jesus' all to trusting simplicity should bring us joy, not become a law that ucks the joy and life out of us. So in practicing simplicity we need o avoid legalism. We also need to be careful that pride doesn't make s think we're spiritually superior to other Christians. Pride is sin whether we're proud of what we have or what we don't have. We can void both these pitfalls by focusing first on God's kingdom which produces an inward reality of simplicity that we can freely and humbly demonstrate in outward lifestyle choices.

MAKING LIFE SIMPLER

Following are some simple suggestions for implementing the spiri-ual practice of simplicity and contentment in your life.[2]

Simplicity and contentment is a spiritual and volitional deci-ion; a matter of a submissive heart and a disciplined mind. Just ike Paul, you can learn to be content by first submitting yourself to Christ. Begin by reaffirming your relationship with God and surren-dering your life to Him. Ask for His guidance in choosing what is mportant and the faith to do so. Spend time in silence and solitude eevaluating your life—your habits, activities, priorities, values, and goals. This would be a very good time to engage in the spiritual practice of journaling. Cooperate with the Spirit's work in your life o develop the inner attitudes of simplicity that will affect how you ive and spend money.

Analyze the way you use your financial resources by reviewing your checkbook entries or debit and credit card statements. Decide how you could reduce spending but still meet your needs; thus, free-ng up resources that could be directed toward other concerns.

Develop a process for differentiating between needs and wants. Consider keeping a journal of how the process affected your purchase decisions. Before you make a purchase ask yourself, *Will I own this thing, or will it own me?* Am I *buying this for its usefulness or status?* Determine to become media/hype proof. No matter what the commercials insinuate, you don't really need the newest gadget; in just a few months it won't be the newest thing anyway.

Rediscover the beauty of God's creation. Take time to stop and smell the roses—literally. You can enjoy those roses, and lots of other beautiful things, without owning them. Take advantage of libraries, parks, and other public recreation areas.

The discipline of simplicity is the conscious act of not being tied to the things of this world. So develop a habit of giving things away—and not just stuff you're tired of. Give away something you love and see if you don't love the sense of liberation and contentment more than you loved that thing.

Our calendars are often as cluttered as our basements and attics. Analyze your calendar and demands made on your time. Decide how you can simplify your schedule, freeing yourself for periods of relaxation and personal spiritual renewal. Shun whatever would distract you from your main goal of putting God's rule first in your life.

Test the practice of simplicity for a predetermined period of time (such as a week or a month) by cutting back on something you do just because you want to (eating out, shopping for nonessentials, having that daily pricey cup of coffee). Tell a friend what you have decided to do. When the time period is over, talk with that friend about the experience and what you learned about godly contentment through the process.

What might be your greatest challenge when it comes to practicing simplicity?

What steps can you take to overcome that challenge?

What is one thing you will do this week to simplify your life?

---

[1] Craig L. Blomberg, "Matthew" in *The New American Commentary*, vol. 22 (Nashville: Broadman Press, 1992), 123.

[2] Some suggestions are adapted and summarized from Richard J. Foster, *Celebration of Discipline: The Path to Spiritual Growth* (New York: HarperOne, 1998), 90-95.

CHAPTER 11

CONFESSION

RESTORING WHOLENESS

Though we can confess our sins directly to God and require no human mediator, there is spiritual power and healing when we confess our sins to one another and pray for each other.

BACKGROUND PASSAGE	FOCAL PASSAGE	MEMORY VERSE
JAMES 5	JAMES 5:13-20	JAMES 5:16a

AN APPROPRIATE EXPRESSION

I have sinned against God, you, and the church," the woman motionally confessed; a person from whom the group least expected o hear such words. Responses varied. Some were uncomfortably ilent. Others angered. A few were indifferent. The vast majority, owever, reached out to her physically with outstretched arms to mbrace her, and spiritually with grace to forgive her. They prayed ogether and committed to give her support in the days ahead. As result, the woman's relationship with Christ and the church was trengthened, and their witness increased in effectiveness.

One appropriate expression of a Christian community is onfessing our sins to one another and praying for spiritual healing or each other. Obviously, we begin by confessing our sins directly o God but divine power is released and spiritual healing results vhen we confess our sins and pray for one another.

CONFESS AND PRAY

James, Jesus' brother and early church leader, wrote to Christians facing external pressure in the form of persecution and internal stress that often accompanies relationships. His letter is filled with practical advice on how to deal with these issues.

According to James 5:13-20 (below), what advice would James offer if you sought his counsel about pressures in your life?

> 13 *Is anyone among you suffering? He should pray. Is anyone*
> *cheerful? He should sing praises.* 14 *Is anyone among you sick?*
> *He should call for the elders of the church, and they should pray*
> *over him after anointing him with olive oil in the name of the*
> *Lord.* 15 *The prayer of faith will save the sick person, and the Lord*
> *will restore him to health; if he has committed sins, he will be*
> *forgiven.* 16 *Therefore, confess your sins to one another and pray*
> *for one another, so that you may be healed. The urgent request of*
> *a righteous person is very powerful in its effect.* 17 *Elijah was a*
> *man with a nature like ours; yet he prayed earnestly that it would*
> *not rain, and for three years and six months it did not rain on*
> *the land.* 18 *Then he prayed again, and the sky gave rain and the*
> *land produced its fruit.* 19 *My brothers, if any among you strays*
> *from the truth, and someone turns him back,* 20 *let him know*
> *that whoever turns a sinner from the error of his way will save his*
> *life from death and cover a multitude of sins.*

A RESPONSIVE COMMUNITY

Life has ups and downs; highs and lows. We know suffering, joy, an anguish. As he brought his letter to a close, James reminded believers we can experience Christ's victory in all circumstances when we pray and do life together in community.

hat do you do first and last when difficulties come into your fe?

irst:

ast:

irst, James addressed those **suffering** from troubles such as ersecution, misfortunes that result from living in a fallen world, or ven slander by a fellow believer. How should we respond? Some hoose to fight back and end up charting a course as evil as the one at befell them. Others are so overwhelmed they retreat, resigned accept what is. Still others whine and complain about their istreatment. James had another idea: **pray** and seek divine interention to change the situation or power and mercy to endure it.

When we are facing trouble, we are prone to pray. When things e going well, we may not pray as much. But joyous occasions are ot to be taken for granted but celebrated. So in **cheerful** times elievers **should sing praises.**

James offered instructions for how the Christian community to respond to physical illness. The sick person **should call for he elders of the church** who were to **pray over him after nointing him with olive oil**. Some think anointing with oil efers to medical treatment that is to accompany praying. Others ink it is an outward sign representing the power of prayer being pplied" to the life of the sick one. While not denying the legitiacy of the literal application of the practice, neither do we want to veremphasize it. The oil did not have the power to heal; James was ot suggesting some magic potion. Both the praying and anointing ere to be done **in the name of the Lord**, for therein lay the ue power and authority of their act.

The prayer of faith rendered by **the elders of the hurch** serving as extensions of the community of faith **will save he sick person**. *Save* comes from a word that also means to heal r make whole. James was writing in the context of physical healing, ot spiritual salvation. The effectiveness of prayers for healing is not ependent on saying the right formula; it is found in the attitude of ith with which it is offered. James had already noted trust in God was essential to prayer (1:5-8; 4:1-3). Note in this case the faith is that of the ones praying. Nothing is said about the faith of the sick person. James stressed the **Lord will restore him to health**. Healing is the act of a sovereign Lord who chooses when and how t answer prayer.

In addition, **if he has committed sins, he will be forgiven** (v. 15b). *If* is a key word in this phrase. Sin may or may not be an underlying cause for the sickness. However, the elders' prayers provided opportunity for the sick person to confess any known sin. The elders were not to demand such a confession or assume one was needed.

Some would suggest that verse 15 is a blanket promise that praying in faith will always result in healing from sickness. Others would suggest the failure to be healed is due to insufficient faith. These are troubling issues beyond the scope of this study but deserv ing brief comment. Over the centuries multitudes of people who were prayed for by Christ's community either were not restored to full health or died from their illness. The prayer of faith for healing must be a prayer of faith that believes God does all things well. Prayer is to be offered by believers but will be answered by the Father in the context of His purpose, which is not always fully explained to us.

What role can you play in helping your Christian community respond appropriately to those who are—

Suffering?

Joyful?

Physically ill?

A CONFESSING COMMUNITY

James moved from talking about physical healing to the more essen tial spiritual healing that repairs a believer's relationships with God and others. He described times when members of a faith community **confess** their **sins** publicly **to one another** (v. 16), such s grudges, resentments, judgmental attitudes, and even deliberate ctions taken to harm or inflict pain on the body.

Confession without prayer misses the point of confession. ʒelievers are to receive the confessional information to prepare hem to pray. They can then **pray for one another** asking for ɔod's reconciling work to take place within the fellowship **so that ou may be healed**, or restored to wholeness. **You** is plural; thus reference to the entire fellowship of believers.

ɔompare James 5:16a with 1 Timothy 2:5. Are these verses ontradictory or complementary? Explain.

esus bought forgiveness for our sins and is the only mediator etween sinful humanity and God. We do not and cannot go hrough anyone else to have our sins forgiven. But there are times vhen we have repeatedly prayed for forgiveness but just could ıot shake the guilt or recurring habit of sin. This is when we can ngage in the rich spiritual practice of corporate confession. When ellow believers respond with grace, prayer, and assurances of God's omplete forgiveness, they become a visible and verbal expression of Jesus in our lives and make His forgiveness real to us.

ɪow might corporate confession benefit you and help you laim victory over sin?

Vhat barriers might prevent you from confessing sin to other elievers?

Vhat would it take for you to overcome those barriers?

PRAYING COMMUNITY

ɔonfession and prayer is not a futile religious exercise but a powerful spiritual practice. We can and must pray urgently for those aught up in sin because **The urgent request of a righteous**

person is very powerful in its effect (v. 16b). A *righteous person* is not a perfect person, but simply someone who has taken right actions to be in right relationship with God. The prayer of such a person is *very powerful in its effect*. The word translated *powerfu[l]* relates directly to the English word "energy." Prayer both energizes the one praying and releases spiritual energy from the Father as He responds to it.

We sometimes say, "Prayer works." That is not exactly what James said. "Prayer is not *itself* powerful; it is not magic. But its powe[r] is unlimited in that the child of God calls on a Father of unlimited goodness and ability."[1] In response, God works in compliance with His purpose. The power in prayer may not always be seen in changing a situation but in God's changing us so we come into agreement with Him, even when we lack understanding. To illustrate His point James referred to the prophet Elijah who had his flaws and weaknesses but still his earnest praying was effective. (See 1 Kings 17:1–18:46.) God does not just hear and respond to the prayers of so-called "super saints;" His ear is attentive to all who come before Him in righteousness.

A REDEMPTIVE COMMUNITY

Confession and prayer are focused on redemption of the sinner and healing of the fellowship. How should the church respond when a fellow believer **strays from the truth** (v. 19)? While the time might come when the offender is cut off from the body, that would be a final action, not the beginning point. James seemed to favor an action whereby **someone turns him back** from his wayward path. The community of faith that prays for healing of the sick surely ought to make every effort to lead a fallen brother or sister to repentance and restoration.

Whoever turns a sinner from the error of his way will save his life from death and cover a multitude of sins. Some think the phrase *will save his life* refers to the person who is acting to restore. In that scenario the person reaching out to restore the one who has strayed would bring salvation to himself and build up a cache of forgiveness to apply to future failures on his part. That understanding is highly inconsistent with the New Testament message. We do not earn or store up favor with God by what we do. Therefore, *will save his life* is to be understood to refer to the one who had strayed but was being restored. When he repents and confesses his sins to the Lord, the Lord will forgive, his spiritually broken life will be made whole, and his sins will be covered by God's forgiving grace. His sins will be forgotten by the Lord and should also be forgotten by his brothers and sisters in Christ in the sense that they will not be held up to the person as a reminder of the past, to rebuke him in the present, or to threaten him in the future. "The person is not branded in the church as someone who once went astray but is part of a company in which all are forgiven sinners."[2]

We can see this principle in King David's life. His adulterous relationship with Bathsheba and attempt to cover the sin by having her husband killed in battle are a dark period in David's life. When the prophet Nathan confronted David with his sin, he confessed, "I have sinned against the LORD." Nathan assured David, "The LORD has taken away your sin; you will not die" (2 Sam. 12:13). While David had to face the consequences of his sin, because of his confession and by the Lord's mercy, He was not lost to service. God restored him to favor and continued to use him mightily.

Confession requires the sinner to be appropriately vulnerable and demands those who hear the confession to consider it a sacred trust that will not become a topic of discussion (gossip) at the next gathering. The fellowship among believers ought to be a safe place where a person can be open and honest. While there is a need for trained professionals in dealing with some issues related to bringing a person back to a life of truth, what James was concerned with is developing authentic community where appropriate transparency and vulnerability allows believers to confess their sins to one another and experience redemptive healing.

What would it take for the small groups you are involved in to be a safe place for believers to be transparent about their sins?

What can you do to help create that atmosphere of safety?

THAT YOU MAY BE HEALED

The spiritual practice of corporate confession recognizes the church is a community of sinners all in need of ongoing transformation. As we confess our faults to one another, our fellow Christians become a tangible expression of God who hears our confession and offers forgiveness. There is freedom and release in the discipline of confession.

Corporate confession, when practiced biblically, is beneficial for everyone. Revealing our failures and weaknesses to others excises the poison of pride in our lives and clears the way for true healing to occur. When we confess our struggles with sin to sincere believers who will pray for us and come alongside us on our journey, we are released from a heavy load of pretense and guilt. Summoning the courage to obey Christ when He tells you to confess a sin publicly cannot only transform you, but also other believers. Hearing you confess your sin and praying for your healing could be just the encouragement others need to leave forgiven failures in the past and press forward on their journey toward Christlikeness.

Confession is certainly a gift of God's grace in that when we confess our sins, He *is faithful and righteous to forgive us our sins and to cleanse us from all unrighteousness* (1 John 1:9). But corporate confession is also a spiritual practice in that there are specific things we can do.

Determine to be vulnerable and transparent with one or more trusted believers. This might mean finding an accountability partner with whom you can share ongoing struggles, confess sin, and count on to pray for you. It may mean being willing to drop the mask and be real with your small group. You don't need to, nor probably should, give all the details of your sin but you can share your sorrow at being self-centered rather than Christ-centered and at being conformed to the world rather than living like one who is being transformed into the image of Jesus. If you don't have anyone you feel you can trust to hear your confession, follow James' advice and pray. Ask God to reveal to you that person or group you can trust to lovingly listen to you and hold you accountable.

The corporate practice of confession calls for you not only to be willing to confess your sins, but also to be a trusted person that others can come to with their confession. People will most likely see you as a safe person when you've been transparent with your own struggles. We seem to be more comfortable sharing with others who've tripped a few times on their own journey.

An absolute requirement in hearing another's confession is complete confidentiality—do not divulge to anyone what that person has told you and refuse to talk about it with others who also heard that confession.

A person confessing their sins to you is being honest, so you must be honest as well. Don't brush off a confession with statements such as, "Oh, that's not such a big deal. Don't worry about it." Agree with them that it's sin and help them to see true repentance is not just asking for forgiveness but also turning their back on that sin and refusing to allow it to be a life habit anymore. Be understanding rather than condescending. Be shockproof by realizing you also are a sinner who has missed God's mark. Listen. Don't be quick to give advice or comfort. Don't be afraid of silence—it might be just what that person needs to dig down deep and share the real sin-sickness that is tearing them up. Encourage them by sharing verses about God's complete forgiveness.

What word pictures do the following verses use to describe God's forgiveness? Which word picture is the most meaningful to you and why?

Psalm 103:12

Isaiah 43:25

Micah 7:18-19

Whatever else you do with a person who is confessing their sins to you, pray. Pray they see Christ's love and grace shining out of you. Pray they will be able to share the real issue. Pray with them that they will experience and rejoice in the genuine healing and release of God's forgiveness.

As you journey toward Christlikeness, understand corporate confession is not an indication of weakness but of ever-progressing spiritual maturity. Bringing your faults and sins out into the open before others allows God to do a special work of healing and transformation in your life and theirs.

Prayerfully complete the following statements:

In order to confess my sins to other believers I would need to…

In order to be the kind of person others feel safe confessing to I would need to…

---

[1] Peter H. Davids, "James" *Understanding the Bible Commentary Series* (Grand Rapids, MI: Baker Books, 1989), 125.
[2] Ibid, 127.

CHAPTER 12

MAKING DISCIPLES

REPLICATING THE GOSPEL IN OTHERS

WHY STUDY THIS LESSON? We are not only called to be disciples of Jesus but we're also called to make disciples of Jesus. As Jesus taught the truth of God, demonstrated life in God, and replicated this truth in others, we must do the same.

BACKGROUND PASSAGE	FOCAL PASSAGE	MEMORY VERSE
2 TIMOTHY 2:1-13	2 TIMOTHY 2:1-2	2 TIMOTHY 2:2

LOOKING LIKE JESUS

The family enjoyed looking through old photographs at grandmother's house. The younger children were fascinated by their parents' and grandparents' clothing and hairstyles. "How could anyone possibly dress like that? And what about that hair!" they howled with delight. As Mom and Dad looked at themselves in some of those pictures, they silently wondered the same thing.

Something else stood out as the family viewed the pictures. Had it not been for the quality of the photographs, it would have been difficult to distinguish one generation of baby pictures from another. They noticed physical features and traits that transcended the generations. Everyone began to see some of their ancestors in themselves.

Jesus is our spiritual ancestor. When others look at us, they ought to see traits in us that remind them of Him. Our desire ought to be to look more and more like Him. One way we can resemble our Savior, who called and made disciples, is to engage in the spiritual practice of disciple-making—leading others to follow Christ—and discipling—guiding others to grow spiritually to conform to His image. While both are a work of the Spirit, followers of Christ have a role in the process. God has called disciples to make disciples. Just as Jesus taught the truth of God, demonstrated life in God, and replicated His truth and life in others, we are to do the same.

In what ways have you progressively conformed to the image of Christ since you first professed faith in Him?

How are you more like Christ today than you were this time last year?

Who or what has helped you make the journey toward transformation?

A MINISTRY OF MULTIPLICATION

The older apostle Paul wrote to his much younger protégé, Timothy, to instruct and encourage him in his ministry to the church at Ephesus. At the time of the writing of his second letter to Timothy, Paul was in prison in Rome. There is an urgency and poignancy in this letter not present in all of Paul's other letters since he was convinced "the time for (his) departure is close" (4:6). It is against this backdrop that Paul offered numerous challenges to Timothy. These were not small challenges. (See 2 Tim. 1:6,8,13-14 for a few examples.) They would demand Timothy's personal best, but Paul knew even that would not be sufficient. He pointed Timothy to a source of strength and gave him some advice for continuing his ministry even in changing times and situations.

ead 2 Timothy 2:1-2 below. What did Paul want Timothy to nake a priority in his ministry?

1 You, therefore, my son, be strong in the grace that is in Christ Jesus. 2 And what you have heard from me in the presence of many witnesses, commit to faithful men who will be able to teach others also.

TRENGTHENED THROUGH GRACE

ecause he considered death imminent, Paul asked Timothy to ome soon because he wanted to see him one more time (1:4; 4:9,21). he bond between the two was great, as is evidenced by Paul's call- ng Timothy **my son**. It is not difficult to imagine if Timothy were resent at Paul's execution that Paul would be offering instruction nd encouragement to him to the very end. In Paul's mind, even hough he was about to be executed, Timothy was the one who vould need encouragement because he was going to continue his ninistry on this earth.

)o you have a relationship with someone similar to the one aul had with Timothy?

Vho is that person?

re you the Paul or Timothy in the relationship?

herefore—because of the demands and expectations placed on imothy and because of the great call that had been given him by he Lord—Paul urged Timothy, **Be strong in the grace that is n Christ Jesus**. Not only would Timothy need to be strong; he lso could be strong. Paul was not laying out an impossible chal- enge or inviting Timothy to try something new. Actually, Paul was rging Timothy "to keep on being strong." The strength he would eed and could claim would be readily available to him as it had een all along. When God gives a person a task to do, He also gives im the strength to do it.

The strength he needed would be *in* (through, by) *the grace that is* located *in Christ Jesus. Grace* is God's unmerited favor; His desire to give what is not deserved and cannot be earned. We come into right relationship with God by His grace; we cannot do it ourselves. We also live by His grace; we can't do it on our own. We will reach heaven by His grace; we won't do that by our own effort either. From beginning to end, grace is extended to us through Christ Jesus. Becoming a disciple is a work of God's grace. Being able to make disciples also is a work of God's grace.

Why would being engaged in making disciples require God's strength and grace?

TEACHING THE GOSPEL

A disciple is a person who submits to and learns from a master teacher. To be a Christian disciple, therefore, is to learn from Jesus. The mandate of Jesus to His followers was "make disciples" (Matt. 28:19). Disciple-making is teaching others the truth of Christ that they too may learn of Him and submit to Him. That would be accomplished, at least in part, by "teaching them to observe everything I have commanded" (Matt. 28:20). Paul was greatly concerned that this teaching would stand on the pure truth of God's Word.

Paul knew he had been a faithful preacher and teacher of the gospel, so he could confidently urge Timothy to recall **what you heard from me**. Hearing in this sense is more than an audible process; it is an experience of the heart and mind. It is receiving information concerning the gospel and being transformed into the image of Christ by the power of the Holy Spirit.

Who first taught you the message of the gospel and how did they do it?

Paul was not the only teacher Timothy had known. His first teachers had been his mother and grandmother. Others also had contributed to his learning the Scriptures and gospel message (2 Tim. 1:5; 3:14-15). The phrase **in the presence of many witnesses** (v.

may suggest what Paul had taught had been confirmed by others ho joined in communicating the truth to Timothy as well. Another ew is that this phrase means part of the way Timothy learned from ul was listening to him teach others. In those settings, Timothy ould have heard the message in detail over and over again so that e doctrines of the faith became well formulated in his heart and ind. Whichever interpretation one chooses, the gospel was not a ivately held message. It was public and widely known by some ho embraced it and others who rejected it.

NTRUSTING THE GOSPEL

1:14, Paul instructed Timothy to "guard, through the Holy irit who lives in us, that good thing entrusted to you." The good ing was the "sound teaching" he had heard from Paul (1:13). The spel that first had been entrusted to Paul (1:12) also had been trusted—deposited or consigned to faithful keeping—to Timo y. Both Paul and Timothy had a stewardship assignment from e Lord to guard the gospel from opponents who would twist or isuse it.

Timothy left for Rome as Paul requested, how would the spel message be guarded and transmitted in Ephesus?

ul had a plan for assuring the continuation of the Lord's work in phesus. Timothy was to **commit** the gospel message **to faithul men** (v. 2b). *Commit* comes from the same word family as the ord *entrust*, meaning "to deposit as a trust for protection." But was not to be entrusted to just anyone, but to *faithful men*. Just ho these men were is not clear. Some believe this refers to some ind of apostolic succession and these instructions are for ministry ofessionals. Nothing in the language supports such a view. Others ink these faithful men were elders of the church appointed under imothy's direction.

Position or title was not the requirement here, however. The ssential qualifier was that they were *faithful*, the kind of people ho could be counted on to discharge their duties fully and in the right way. The gospel must not be placed in the hands of those who desired to be teachers but "don't understand what they are saying or what they are insisting on" (1 Tim. 1:7). Paul did not want Timothy to choose a person who teaches "other doctrine and does not agree with the sound teaching of our Lord Jesus Christ" (1 Tim, 6:3). Moreover, he must stay away from those "who imagine that godliness is a way to material gain" (1 Tim. 6:5).

The word for *men* can also be understood as human beings, whether male or female. Applied in the broadest sense, in our day faithful men and women are needed to care for the gospel as the sacred trust it is.

Would Timothy have chosen you as one of the faithful people to whom he would entrust the gospel?

Yes, because

No, because

I'm not sure because

REPLICATING THE GOSPEL

Kingdom ministry is a ministry of replication by multiplication. That was the kind of ministry Paul desired for Timothy. Those to whom the gospel was committed were to be far more than caretakers. They were not to be satisfied to sit on the treasure box, but to open it carefully and distribute it appropriately that it might have its full effect on those who received it. Those to whom the gospel was to be committed needed to be trustworthy believers **who will be able to teach others also** (v. 2c). *Able* implies competence. To *teach* is to instruct, explain, and expound. Not everyone may be able to teach in the formal sense and the church does well not to try to make teachers of those who are not so gifted.

What Bible teachers or leaders have influenced you the most?

:ow did they contribute to you becoming a disciple of Christ ıd your ongoing spiritual development?

isciple-making and discipling is the singular process of replicat- ıg the gospel in others so they become more like Christ in spirit, titude, and practice. "The kingdom advances one person through ıother person until the gospel is spread throughout the earth. . . . ıe greatest legacy of ministry we can have is to multiply ourselves, ır gospel, our faith, and our ministries in other faithful persons ho will one day do the same."[1] And where do we find the power, rength, and ability to carry out this task? It comes by being "strong the grace that is in Christ Jesus" (2 Tim. 2:1).

ven if you are not a formal Bible teacher, what are you doing share the gospel message with others and to help them ecome more like Christ?

PICTURE OF DISCIPLE-MAKING

the first several verses of Paul's first letter to the believers in the wn of Thessalonica, Paul commended them for their acceptance ıd faithfulness to the gospel (1 Thess. 1:5-10). He reminded them their initial encounter with the gospel through the ministry Paul, Silas, and Timothy. These three followers of Christ had odeled the faith before them. Thus, the gospel became more than ords they spoke, it was proven to be a way of living through the ɔwer of the Holy Spirit at work in them.

ead 1 Thessalonians 1:5-7. Describe the discipling process ıat occurred among the Thessalonians.

Here is the linkage. Paul himself imitated Christ and modeled it before the Thessalonians, who then imitated Christ as they had come to know Him through Paul. The Thessalonians, in turn, modeled the effects of the gospel to other believers far and wide. Their influence became so vast Paul declared, "For the Lord's message rang out from you, not only in Macedonia and Achaia, but in every place that your faith in God has gone out. Therefore, we don't need to say anything" (v. 8). That is a picture of disciple-making and discipling others.

Every believer can be in that picture. Disciple-making and discipling is not an assignment given to a select few specialists; every follower of Christ has been commissioned to this crucial and fulfilling task. Disciple-making includes evangelism, announcing the good news of Jesus, and encouraging a person to choose to follow and learn about Christ. Discipling the new believer is the continuing process in which a mature believer teaches, assists, encourages, and mentors the new follower of Christ to be progressively transformed into the likeness of Christ. The effects of being like Jesus in attitudes and actions will be evident in their homes, places of work and even where they play and relax.

BECOMING A DISCIPLE-MAKER

We all influence other people. Hopefully the more we have become Christ-centered as we've engaged in spiritual practices, the more we have positively influenced others to begin and/or continue the journey toward Christlikeness. However, the spiritual practice of disciple-making goes further than just being a good influence on others. Like all the spiritual practices, disciple-making occurs by determined choices rather than default. The spiritual practice of disciple-making calls for an intentional investment into one or more people for the purpose of guiding or journeying with them toward maturity in the faith.

The first step in this practice is to prepare yourself to be a disciple-maker and a disciple by committing to the spiritual practices that will lead you to becoming more like Christ. We cannot lead someone to be what we do not know or what we are not. Then ıke the initiative to discover those people God wants you to invest ı so you can experience the joy of watching them being progres-vely transformed into the image of Christ.

Here are some suggested ways to practice disciple-making—be Spiritual Friend, Spiritual Mentor, Coach, or Spiritual Director.[2]

A **Spiritual Friend** relationship is between friends who ıare a common spirituality and maturity level. This relationship, ased on mutual love and respect, intentionally focuses on help-ıg each other move progressively deeper in knowing, loving, and ːrving God. Spiritual friendship involves trust, prayer, and focused ialogue on God and His Word.

A **Spiritual Mentor** relationship involves a mature believer ntering into an intentional relationship for the purpose of disci-ling a younger, less spiritually mature believer in knowing and ɔplying God's truths. This relationship involves accountability, ncouragement, and empowerment. When you choose to be a ɔiritual mentor you share with another the experience and wisdom ɔu've gained on your journey.

Based on your own spiritual maturity and skill set you may ıoose to be a **Coach** (in the spiritual, not athletic, sense) who elps a believer discover what he/she already knows and assists ıem to apply that knowledge to take the next steps forward. Coach-ıg involves a lot of listening, helping the mentee think in new ays and form a plan of action, and then giving them the confi-ence to put that plan into action.

A **Spiritual Director** is a prayer partner, listener, and ncourager who helps a disciple develop spiritual eyes and ears to nderstand and obey where God is leading in life and ministry.

If your church has a disciplining or mentoring ministry, make ɔurself available for an assignment. If no ministry exists, consider eing the catalyst for beginning one. Always keep in mind that ngaging in the practice of disciple-making is more than taking or ːading a course at church. Disciple-making and discipling are spiri-ıal actions, for only the Holy Spirit calls one to salvation and brings ɔout spiritual transformation. We are privileged to be allowed to ɔin Him in that work in another's life.

Whether you choose to engage in disciple-making by being a ːllow traveler with a friend or by being a personal guide for another's journey as their mentor, you will need to intentionally invest yourself and your time in the relationship. Establish a consistent time to meet at least monthly and stay in contact throughout each week. Keep in mind the goal of the relationship is to help another believer be a more committed disciple of Jesus who is serious about progressing toward Christlikeness and who will intentionally choose to invest in discipling others.

Disciple-making and discipling are ongoing ventures commissioned by the Lord. In giving the commission He promised His presence until the end of the age (Matt. 28:20). His commission and promised presence remain in effect until He comes again. That in turn, allows believers to be strong in His grace and commit the gospel message to faithful believers who then will be able to teach others.

To whom are you being a mentor or discipler?

What approach are you taking with that person?

If you are not actively making disciples, what do you need to do to become involved?

---

[1] James T. Draper, Jr. and Gene Mims, *The Church Anticipating the Kingdom's Appearing: Studies in 1 & 2 Timothy*, Expository Notes and Leader Helps, January Bible Study, 2004 (Nashville: LifeWay Press, 2003), 60.

[2] For more details on these disciple-making approaches, go to BrentwoodBaptist.com/mentor.

CHAPTER 13

SPIRITUAL TRANSFORMATION

BECOMING LIKE HIM

HY STUDY THIS LESSON? God's great goal in the life of a believer is to conform us into the image of His Son. Every spiritual discipline we practice has the aim of transforming our character so that we are more like Jesus.

BACKGROUND PASSAGE	FOCAL PASSAGE	MEMORY VERSE
NS 12:1-2; 2 CORINTHIANS 3:7-18	ROMANS 12:1-2; 2 CORINTHIANS 3:18	ROMANS 12:2

KEEP MOVING FORWARD

/e left early one Monday morning on a road trip that would onclude at the Grand Canyon. I had mapped out the route antici-ating the miles we could comfortably drive per day, made hotel eservations at the cities we would visit along the way, and investi-ated various sights to explore. For the most part we followed our inerary, but there were a few diversions, detours, and decisions that d us to alter our schedule or change our plans. Some of the reasons at led to change were not to our liking; such as long delays caused y highway construction or losing our way because we decided to et off the well-marked highway. Along the way we also saw some eautiful sights, both those that were part of our travel plan and thers that were completely unexpected. When we finally reached ur destination, we found it to exceed our greatest expectations.

For several weeks we have journeyed together in a study of piritual practices. We had a definite starting point and we had some idea where we were headed and how long it would take us to get there. The study plan was mapped out for us. Perhaps along the way you faced some things that diverted your attention—after all, life goes on in ways we don't always anticipate—yet you have continue[d] the journey. Perhaps you have also had some spiritual experiences you did not anticipate and that exceeded your expectations.

How would you evaluate this study's contribution to your ow[n] spiritual development?

What detours or obstacles have you encountered as you journeyed through this study?

What are some lasting effects you anticipate from participating in this study?

With this session, our Venture Up study is complete, but that does not mean the journey is over. So, keep moving forward—and enjoy the journey.

BE AND BEING TRANSFORMED

In addition to being a letter to the believers at Rome, many conside[r] the Book of Romans to be Paul's theological masterpiece that explains the need, effect, and benefits of the gospel.

As you read this sampling of key verses, ask and answer how each verse contributed to your understanding of salvation an[d] the spiritual transformation journey.

Romans 1:18

Romans 3:23

Romans 5:8

Romans 8:1

Romans 10:9-10

Beginning with chapter 12 Paul turned his attention to the practical applications of the gospel in the life of the believer. Verses 1-2 help connect what Paul had said with the challenges he was about to unfold.

> *1 Therefore, brothers, by the mercies of God, I urge you to present*
> *your bodies as a living sacrifice, holy and pleasing to God; this*
> *is your spiritual worship. 2 Do not be conformed to this age, but*
> *be transformed by the renewing of your mind, so that you may*
> *discern what is the good, pleasing, and perfect will of God*
> *(Rom. 12:1-2).*

Second Corinthians 3:18 is the conclusion of a complex argument in which Paul defended the superiority of the new covenant in Christ over the old covenant of the Law. Because the new covenant is superior, Paul argued, his apostolic ministry had validity and authenticity in spite of what his detractors and critics said. However, the verse also can be applied to all believers. That is how we will focus our attention on the verse.

> *18 We all, with unveiled faces, are looking as in a mirror at the*
> *glory of the Lord and are being transformed into the same image*
> *from glory to glory; this is from the Lord who is the Spirit*
> *(2 Cor. 3:18).*

All of these verses hold in common the concept of spiritual transformation. However, Paul presents two perspectives on what it means. In Romans 12:2, Paul spoke of spiritual transformation as a mandate: **be transformed**. In 2 Corinthians 3:18, he spoke of spiritual transformation as a current event: **are being transformed.**

How would you reconcile those two verses? Is spiritual transformation a one-time event or an ongoing process?

How would you define spiritual transformation to a new believer?

Consider this definition of spiritual transformation. "Spiritual transformation is God's work of changing a believer into the likeness of Jesus by creating a new identity in Christ and by empowering a lifelong relationship of love, trust, and obedience to glorify God."[1] Spiritual transformation is a definitive act of God in Christ. However, spiritual transformation also is an ongoing experience in the believer's life as he or she becomes more like Christ.

BE TRANSFORMED (Rom. 12:1-2)

The word **therefore** in Romans 12:1 serves to lead the reader back to all that had been said in chapters 1–11. The challenge Paul was about to give the Roman believers was to be understood in light of **the mercies**—the longings and compassion—**of God** he had explained to them. Without their knowing and understanding the gospel, what he would say next to the Roman believers wouldn't have much meaning. A believer cannot live like a believer unless he or she has in truth become one. However, if a person is truly a believer in the gospel of Christ, then what he or she professes will become evident in the quality and character of the life being lived.

Looking back, how do you see God's mercies being active in your initial decision to follow Christ?

Consistency between profession and practice was important to Paul, as is seen in his words **I urge you**. *Urge* can be understood as admonish, instruct, exhort, beg—all strong words that suggest this is critical, not something to be ignored. The appeal is that believers **present** their **bodies as a living sacrifice**. God was no longer interested in animal sacrifices, religious ritual, or the gift of things. *Bodies* can be understood as a reference to physical existence, but in this context, it more likely represents our entire personhood.

God does not want a part of your life; He desires all of it. Unless we give God all, the word *sacrifice* has no meaning—for nothing sacrificial has occurred. *Living* may be understood in contrast to dead animal sacrifices or it may be understood in the sense of the new life believers have by the Spirit of God. Either way suggests a life that differs from what had been known. Ordinarily sacrifices lon't *present* themselves to be sacrificed. Here is a reminder that erving Christ is a matter of the will; a person chooses to do so.

While on your spiritual journey, in what ways have you presented yourself as a living sacrifice to the Lord?

As you continue progressing further in your spiritual journey, what is God now asking you to sacrifice?

The sacrifice believers are to make in serving the Lord is to be **holy and pleasing to God**. The root meaning of the word *holy* means o set apart. It is the same word from which "saint" is derived. A saint s a person who has been set aside to the Lord, an act that takes place n Christ. Anything set aside unto the Lord takes and reflects His ighteous nature. A person is not naturally righteous. Only the Lord can make a person righteous. *Pleasing* means to be accepted by, to bring pleasure to. When we choose to serve the Lord we are setting ourselves aside to Him for His purpose and for His good pleasure. This has obvious implications on behavior. The behavior of the believer is to be pleasing to God.

This is your spiritual worship. *Spiritual* comes from a word that means logical, reasonable. *Worship* is service given to the Lord; it is no longer ritual obligation. Therefore, giving yourself as a sacrifice to the Lord is the most reasonable service to render. It is the least you should do. It is what is expected of you.

Are you satisfied that your way of behaving pleases and serves the Lord? Why or why not?

Where do you need to make changes?

The logical decision to give self to the worship and service of the Lord would lead to another definitive action, which Paul stated negatively. **Do not conform to this age**. By *this* age Paul meant the period while living in a world polluted by sin. To *conform* is to shape something according to an established pattern. In and of itself, "conform" is a neutral word. What one conforms to is the issue. In this case, Paul exhorted believers not to make the established patterns of a sinful world the standard by which they were shaped. This was not a call to separatism. Believers cannot influence a world order they are not willing to engage. However, believers are to be cautious; not allowing the engagement to lead to accepting and conforming to what the world considers to be normal thinking and behavior.

In which areas of life do you often feel the greatest pressure to conform to the standards and practices promoted by popular culture?

How do you most often handle that pressure?

Rather than conforming, believers are to **be transformed.** The word *transformed* comes from the same word as the English word *metamorphosis*, which means to change from one form to another. Applied spiritually, the change is not merely external. It is an internal change that comes **by the renewing of your mind**. It is the result of a complete renovation of the way you think, your moral perception and understanding.

Only then can a person **discern what is the good, pleasing, and perfect will of God**. To *discern* is to test the worth of something. In this case, it is the ability to test and prove that God's will, which includes His purpose and desire for His children, is what is best for us, acceptable to God, and lacking in nothing that would prevent it from accomplishing its full intent. Paul was urging the believers to conform, but this time, to the will of God. God's will and purpose was to be the standard that shaped their lives, both what they thought and how they behaved.

BEING TRANSFORMED (2 Cor. 3:18)

In the larger argument beginning in 2 Corinthians 3:7, Paul had used the image of veiled faces as a way to refer to the hardness of eart and spiritual blindness of those who refused the new covenant n Christ. In contrast, believers in Christ have **unveiled faces** nd are able to see clearly the things of God. The image is of **looking as in a mirror** and seeing a reflection of **the glory of the Lord**. His glory can be seen in creation, in His Word, in worship, nd even in the acts of loving-kindness toward us by our brothers nd sisters in Christ. Of course, the greatest revelation of God's ower and brilliance is Christ Jesus.

When have you seen or experienced the glory of the Lord—a manifestation of His presence with power and brilliance?

What lasting effect did it have on you?

One Bible teacher provides an interesting explanation behind the mage of looking in a mirror. "It was the property of mirrors back in hose days (which were made of a flat, circular piece of cast metal) hat the more polished the surface, the clearer the image. Continuous elbow grease was needed to keep away corrosion. The picture is provocative one. The life and ministry of the believer are depicted s a mirror that is in need of continual polishing so as to reproduce o an ever-increasing extent the glorious knowledge and truths of he gospel."[2]

As believers we cannot stand face to face with the glory of he Lord and not be changed. We cannot stand in the presence of Christ without being affected. In every encounter with Him and His glory we **are being transformed into the same image from glory to glory.** The verb tense means this is an ongoing process. The words *same image* remind us of the creation account where humankind was created in the image of God. That image was marred by sin. However, because of what Christ has done and our experience in Him, we are being restored to the image God ntended in the beginning; an image that reflects His holiness and righteousness. We have been made anew, recreated, and reborn. Another view is that the words mean we are being transformed to he image of Christ—becoming like Christ; reflecting Christ. The phrase *from glory to glory* suggests this is an ever-increasing experience; we grow more and more into God's glory; we become more and more like Christ.

If the Corinthian believers were overwhelmed by the challenge of becoming more and more like Christ, Paul had a word to set them—and us—at ease. **This is from the Lord who is the Spirit.** "But just as we cannot save ourselves, so we cannot change ourselves into His likeness. Only the power of the risen Christ can accomplish genuine and lasting change in us . . . . Through Christ we are changed from one degree of glory to another, until at last we are entirely transformed into his likeness and glory."[3]

When it comes to my spiritual transformation what is:

God's role?

My role?

ROUGH SPOTS AND SPIRITUAL HEIGHTS

Simon Peter is a strong example of one who was spiritually transformed. It was a journey for him, one filled with a few rough spots but also one that took him to spiritual heights. Perhaps that is why we identify with him.

Invest the time to read these Scripture passages that represent some steps in Peter's personal spiritual journey.

- Introduction to Jesus — John 1:40-42
- Response to Christ's call to follow him — Luke 5:1-10
- Faithful and eager — Matthew 14:26-29
- Doubtful and fearful — Matthew 14:30-31
- A great confession — Matthew 16:13-17
- An emphatic denial — John 18:15-17,25-27

• Compassionate restoration	John 21:15-19
• Spirit-filled proclamation	Acts 2:1,14-40
• New perspective	Acts 10
• Living in hope	1 Peter 1:3-9
• Growing in faith	2 Peter 1:3-11
• Spiritual mentor	2 Peter 3:11-18

n what ways do you identify with Peter's journey toward ransformation?

AN ETERNAL ADVENTURE

'he decision to commit our lives to Christ and follow Him is he first step on the journey toward spiritual transformation. The ourney will not end until we gather in the heaven of eternity. In etween, from the journey's beginning to its end, is a life marked by ctive and dynamic spiritual adventure. "Spiritual transformation is process—a progressive change of worldview, values, attitudes, and ehavior. Beginning with the heart and reaching out to touch the ife and witness of God's people at every level, God's Word and God's Spirit bring transformation. Spiritual transformation at its foundaion is a change of the heart that expresses itself in the outward life."[4] n being spiritually transformed believers learn more and more o understand, appreciate, and conform to what it means to be a follower of Christ and bring glory to His name.

After we arrive in heaven the adventure will continue in ways we cannot even imagine. Until then we continue to develop, hrough the Spirit's power, a lifestyle characterized by spiritual habits and practices so we can engage with God, hear from Him, and allow Him to transform us more into the image of Jesus.

Here are some simple suggestions for living as a follower of Christ committed to being continuously spiritually transformed:

- Review the spiritual practices that have been part of the Venture In and Venture Up studies. Identify what each practice means and the value or benefit it has for your spiritual journey. For greater personal understanding and implementation, consider facilitating a small group study of *Venture In* or *Venture Up*.

- In your journal list spiritual practices that have been an ongoing part of your own spiritual journey, practices that you implemented early in your walk with Christ. How did you get started? How have those practices contributed to you growing as a follower of Christ? Why would you commend them to others?
- List a practice or practices that you have begun to include in your spiritual journey since the beginning of this study. Why did you make that choice? What impact did it have on you becoming less self-centered and more Christ-centered? What expectations do you have for what the practice(s) will contribute to your spiritual life?
- Continue your study of spiritual practices by reading *Celebration of Discipline* by Richard J. Foster and *Spiritual Disciplines for the Christian Life* by Donald S. Whitney.
- Draw a spiritual time line that illustrates your journey of being spiritually transformed. Include difficult experiences to which you did not respond well and others that were spiritual mountaintops. Looking back, how did each of those experiences contribute to your spiritual journey?

Complete this prayer:

Lord, at the conclusion of this study on spiritual practices I want to say to You…

---

[1] Jay Johnston and Ronald K. Brown, *Teaching the Jesus Way: Building a Transformational Teaching Ministry* (Nashville: LifeWay Press, 2000), 12.

[2] Linda L. Belleville, "2 Corinthians," *The IVP New Testament Commentary Series*, vol. 8 (Downers Grove, IL: InterVarsity Press, 1996), 112-13.

[3] Ernest Best, "Second Corinthians" *Interpretation: A Bible Commentary for Teaching and Preaching* (Louisville: John Knox Press, 1987), 35.

[4] Johnston and Brown, 55.

COMMITMENT TO THE JOURNEY

Throughout the past weeks, you may have considered recording the commitment God is moving you to make as a response to this study. At that time, perhaps you were not ready—not convinced that it was something you wanted to do just then. You do well to think carefully and prayerfully before making promises to anyone, and especially to God.

But if you have been moved as you've studied these disciplines, and made aware of the potential for changing your faith walk in dynamic and dramatic ways by practicing the disciplines, won't you take a moment right now to ask God for specific direction?

Far from being rituals or obligations—practicing prayer, meditation, study, communing with God through fasting or sacrifice or sharing your faith—are all designed to put you in a position so that God can transform you into the person He designed you to be.

The best news is that God knows our weaknesses and frailties. As our Creator, God well understands the limitations of human effort. In His great mercy and love, God provides the Holy Spirit to guide us, encourage us and sustain us as we launch out in faith. When we take the smallest step of obedience, He runs to meet us in the same way the father joyfully welcomed the prodigal son in Scripture.

In the space provided below, write down what you believe God is calling you to do. It's not the single step, or how many steps you are willing to take that matters. It's that you've determined to invite His transformation through your willing obedience to become more and more like Him!

Today, as a first step (or a new step) in moving forward to a Christ-centered life, I commit to

____.

Signed:______________________________

Date:______________________________

SPIRITUAL PRACTICES OVERVIEW

BY CATEGORY

I. BIBLE
- Reading
- Study
- Memorization
- Meditation

II. COMMUNION WITH GOD
- Prayer
- Journaling
- Solitude and Silence
- Fasting

III. CHARACTER
- Sacrifice
- Love
- Suffering and Perseverance
- Joy and Celebration

IV. STEWARDSHIP
- Giving
- Time
- Gifts and Talents
- Simplicity and Contentment

V. CORPORATE
- Worship
- Fellowship and Community
- Godly Counsel
- Confession

VI. OUTWARD
- Sharing your Faith
- Service
- Missions
- Mentoring / Disciple Making

VENTURE IN

SPIRITUAL PRACTICES
- Bible: Reading
- Communion with God: Prayer
- Character: Sacrifice
- Stewardship: Giving
- Corporate: Worship
- Outward: Sharing your Faith

SPIRITUAL PRACTICES
- Bible: Study
- Communion with God: Journaling
- Character: Love
- Stewardship: Time
- Corporate: Fellowship and Community
- Outward: Service

VENTURE UP

SPIRITUAL PRACTICES
- Bible: Memorization
- Communion with God: Solitude and Silence
- Character: Suffering and Perseverance
- Stewardship: Gifts and Talents
- Corporate: Godly Counsel
- Outward: Missions

SPIRITUAL PRACTICES
- Bible: Meditation
- Communion with God: Fasting
- Character: Joy and Celebration
- Stewardship: Simplicity and Contentment
- Corporate: Confessions
- Outward: Mentoring / Disciple Making

RESOURCES

HELPFUL BOOKS RELATED TO SPIRITUAL PRACTICES AND SPIRITUAL FORMATION

Andrews, Alan, ed. *The Kingdom Life: A Practical Theology of Discipleship and Spiritual Formation.* Colorado Springs: NavPress, 2010.

Boa, Kenneth. *Conformed to His Image: Biblical and Practical Approaches to Spiritual Formation.* Grand Rapids, MI: Zondervan, 2001.

Foster, Richard J. *Celebration of Discipline: The Path to Spiritual Growth.* New York: HarperOne, 1998.

Ortberg, John. *The Life You've Always Wanted: Spiritual Disciplines for Ordinary People.* Grand Rapids, MI: Zondervan, 2002.

Whitney, Donald S. *Spiritual Disciplines for the Christian Life.* Colorado Springs: NavPress, 1991.

Willard, Dallas. *The Spirit of the Disciplines: Understanding How God Changes Lives.* New York: HarperCollins Publishers, 1988.

HELPFUL BOOKS RELATED TO STUDYING THE BIBLE

Fee, Gordon D. and Douglas Stuart. *How to Read the Bible for All Its Worth.* Grand Rapids, MI: Zondervan, 2003.

Guthrie, George H., *Read the Bible for Life - Workbook* (accompanies DVD sessions). Nashville: LifeWay Christian Resources, 2011.

Hendricks, Howard G. and William D. Hendricks. *Living By the Book: The Art and Science of Reading the Bible.* Chicago: Moody Publishers, 2007.

Plummer, Robert. *40 Questions about Interpreting the Bible.* Grand Rapids: Kregel Academic and Professional, 2010.

HELPFUL COMMENTARIES AND OTHER BIBLICAL RESOURCES

Holman Illustrated Bible Dictionary. Nashville: Holman Reference, 2003.

Holman New Testament Commentary Set. Nashville: Broadman & Holman Publishers.

The IVP New Testament Commentary Series. Downers Grove, IL; InterVarsity Press.

The New American Commentary Set. Nashville: Broadman Press.

The New Bible Commentary. Downers Grove, IL: IVP Academic.

HELPFUL WEBSITES FOR BIBLE STUDY

www.MyStudyBible.com | www.biblegateway.com | www.e-sword.net

- Various other resources are referenced in the *Travelogues* and Teaching Plans that are specific to those lessons.

ABOUT THE WRITING TEAM

Ronald K. Brown wrote the 13-lesson series, providing rich biblical study of the selected passages and a sound theological basis for the spiritual practices that are the focus of *Venture Up*.

Since accepting Christ at the age of 10, and his subsequent acceptance of God's call to ministry at the age of 16, Ron has lived out that call in a multitude of settings. He pastored churches in several states for more than 20 years. He served LifeWay Christian Resources, Nashville, Tennessee, as a curriculum editor, Bible study leadership resources editor, *Open Windows* magazine editor, and he completed his 23-year tenure as Senior Managing Director of Leadership and Adult Publishing.

Ron earned a Bachelor of Arts degree at Eastern Michigan University, the Master of Divinity and Doctor of Ministry degrees at The Southern Baptist Theological Seminary, Louisville, Kentucky. He and his wife Connie have two adult children and five grandchildren. The couple currently serves at Pleasant Heights Baptist Church, Columbia, Tennessee.

Amy Tucker Summers contributed interactive questions, illustrative material and practical tools for personal application of spiritual practices introduced in *Venture Up*. Amy is an experienced and skilled writer, drawing learners into Bible truths through relevant and engaging stories, questions and reflections on both their present and potential spiritual habits.

She holds a Bachelor of Arts degree from Baylor University and the Master of Arts in Religious Education degree from Southwestern Baptist Theological Seminary. Her work includes writing adult teaching procedures and personal study guides for *MasterWork*, *Explore the Bible*, *Quick-source*, and *Bible Studies for Life*.

Her real-life experiences as a wife, mother to three children, and her personal commitment to discipling others as an adult Bible study teacher are reflected in her warm, yet probing writing style. She and her husband live in the beautiful Blue Ridge Mountains of western North Carolina where they serve the Trinity of Fairview Baptist Church in Fletcher.

Linda Lawson Still wrote the teaching plans for this study. She has written content and teaching plans for numerous LifeWay Christian Resources publications including *Explore the Bible* Series. She was employed 31 years at LifeWay, retiring in 2002 as Director of Communications.

Linda has been married to her husband, Pat, for 37 years. They are members of ClearView Baptist Church in Franklin, Tennessee, where she is a co-teacher of an adult Bible study class. She is a veteran of more than 25 mission trips in the United States and many foreign countries.

A native of Missouri, Linda accepted Christ as her Savior at the age of eight at First Baptist Church, Jefferson City, Missouri. She is a graduate of William Jewell College in Liberty, Missouri, and holds an M. A. Degree in journalism from the University of Missouri. Since retiring, Linda enjoys freelance writing for Bible study curriculum and feature articles for magazines.

David T. Seay served as content editor for both the Foundations study and the teaching plans on Spiritual Practices. He has a rich and varied background as a church staff member (pastor and minister of education), content editor for Sunday school-related materials at LifeWay Christian Resources, training conference leader, and concluded his 24-plus years at LifeWay as Editor in Chief of *Mature Living* magazine. He served in the U. S. Air Force from 1965-70, achieving the rank of captain.

David holds a Bachelor of Arts degree in journalism from Texas Tech University and a Master of Divinity degree from Southwestern Baptist Theological Seminary. He and his wife Melva reside in Franklin, Tennessee. The couple has two daughters, Laura and Kathryn. Active in his church, Brentwood Baptist, Brentwood, Tennessee, David is a deacon and serves as assistant teacher of an adult Bible class.